Free limited time bonus

Stop for a moment. We have a free bonus set up for you. The problem is this: we forget 90% of everything that we read after 7 days. Crazy fact, right? Here's the solution: we've created a printable, 1-page pdf summary for this book that you're reading now. All you have to do to get your free pdf summary is to go to the following website: **https://livetolearn.lpages.co/enthrallinghistory/**

Once you do, it will be intuitive. Enjoy, and thank you!

Table of Contents

INTRODUCTION 1

PART ONE: FROM THE NEOLITHIC AGE TO THE BRONZE
AGE COLLAPSE (7000 BCE–750 BCE) 3

    CHAPTER 1: THE AGE OF STONE, MINOANS, AND CYCLADIC
    CIVILIZATION 4

    CHAPTER 2: THE MYCENAEANS AND THE DARK AGES 17

PART TWO: FROM THE ARCHAIC YEARS TO ROMAN
CONQUEST (750–146 BCE) 28

    CHAPTER 3: THE ARCHAIC YEARS 29

    CHAPTER 4: CLASSICAL GREECE 40

    CHAPTER 5: PHILIP II AND ALEXANDER THE GREAT 51

    CHAPTER 6: THE DIADOCHI AND THE ROMAN CONQUEST..... 62

PART THREE: THE ROMAN AND BYZANTINE PERIODS
(146 BCE–1453 CE) 74

    CHAPTER 7: THE GRECO-ROMAN WORLD AND EARLY
    BYZANTINE YEARS 75

    CHAPTER 8: BYZANTIUM UNDER GREEK INFLUENCE 87

    CHAPTER 9: LAST YEARS OF BYZANTIUM 99

PART FOUR: NEW AND MODERN GREEK HISTORY
(1453 CE–20TH CENTURY) 110

    CHAPTER 10: OTTOMAN RULE AND THE WAR OF
    INDEPENDENCE 111

    CHAPTER 11: GREECE IN THE 19TH CENTURY 122

History of Greece

An Enthralling Overview of Greek History

CHAPTER 12: GREECE IN THE 20TH CENTURY 132

CONCLUSION 143

HERE'S ANOTHER BOOK BY ENTHRALLING HISTORY THAT
YOU MIGHT LIKE 145

FREE LIMITED TIME BONUS 146

BIBLIOGRAPHY 147

Introduction

The land of Greece and its history captures the imagination. With rugged mountains surrounded by the sea, Greece's history brings to mind epic poetry, elegant sculptures, and the inception of democracy. Greece fought unforgettable wars against the Persian, Roman, and Ottoman Empires, but its internal wars were perhaps the most memorable. For much of its history, Greece was not a single nation but a group of fractious city-states vying for supremacy. Greek settlements spread far beyond today's country of Greece to colonies around the Mediterranean and the Black Sea.

Through nine thousand years of history, several Greek civilizations rose to astounding heights before suffering cataclysmic falls. Ever resilient, new Greek powers rose from the ashes to leave their mark on the world. The Macedonian Empire under Alexander the Great and his successors stretched from the Balkan Peninsula south to Egypt and across Asia to the Indus Valley. The Byzantine Empire later claimed much of this same territory.

Greece influenced the rest of the world, especially Roman culture. But it also absorbed and further developed the scientific knowledge, technologies, and religions of its surrounding regions. This fusion of Asian, North African, and European learning formed the Hellenistic culture, a powerhouse of the arts, sciences, and philosophy. The eastern remnant of the Roman Empire continued for over a millennium as the powerful Byzantine Empire, oriented toward Greek culture and the bastion of Eastern Orthodox

Christianity. Greece's multifaceted and enduring legacy has enriched the world.

This book endeavors to guide you on an understandable, enjoyable journey through Greece's history from the Stone Age to the 20th century. This concise overview will introduce the various Greek civilizations and explain the distinctive features of each era and what made them exceptional. Of course, history isn't just dry facts and dates; it's about people. This book brings their stories to life in all their ingenuity, desperation, bravery, and artistry.

Reading history can be fascinating, but it also has immeasurable benefits. Learning Greece's history helps us understand the Greek foundation for political innovation in recent centuries and how its art and architecture influenced our sense of aesthetics. We are indebted to the Greek historians for not only recording their own history but also the histories of the Babylonians, Persians, Romans, and more. What the Greeks left behind is woven into our lives today.

Let's travel back to Greece's earliest settlements and explore the Greeks' stunning contributions to our world!

PART ONE:
From the Neolithic Age to the Bronze Age Collapse (7000 BCE–750 BCE)

Chapter 1: The Age of Stone, Minoans, and Cycladic Civilization

A skull! The stalagmite growing from its head looked like a horn at first glance. Christos, a Greek villager, bent over for a closer look, focusing his light on the bizarre find in the Petralona Cave. Was it human?

A year earlier, in 1959, a shepherd named Filippos had been scouring the slopes of Mount Katsika in Greece's Chalcidice, a peninsula in northern Greece. He was searching for a water source for his flocks. He discovered an opening to a massive cave. Inside, he found multiple chambers covered with stalactites and stalagmites. And now, Christos found a skull in a small cavern within the cave.

Geologists and paleontologists have investigated the skull and cave for the past six decades. The skull is missing its jawbone but still has its upper teeth. Researchers continue to debate whether the skull is male or female. Is it a *Homo sapien* (modern human) or an earlier ancestor? Just how old is it? The fiercely contested estimates range from 160,000 years old to 700,000. Anthropologists concluded that it possessed European traits, challenging the theory that the first humans emerged out of Africa.

The calcification-covered Petralona skull with a protruding stalagmite.

Geological changes have complicated the archaeological study of Greece's prehistoric Stone Age. The Greek peninsula is located between the African and Eurasian geological plates. For millennia, as Africa slowly moved a centimeter a year toward Greece, the collision of the two plates caused constant geological folding, uplift, volcanoes, and earthquakes. Erosion produced by farmers clearing trees from Greece's mountainous landscape further disrupted the archaeological record.[1]

The Stone Age refers to the earliest period of human existence when ancient people used stone tools. Archaeologists hotly contest the beginning date for this period. Assuming that processes like radiometric decay occurred at today's rates, many scientists estimate a date of two to three million years ago. The ending date was around 3300 BCE when humans began using bronze implements,

---

[1] Curtis Runnels, "Review of Aegean Prehistory IV: The Stone Age of Greece from the Paleolithic to the Advent of the Neolithic," *American Journal of Archaeology* 99, no. 4 (1995): 699. https://doi.org/10.2307/506190.

although various civilizations progressed at different rates.

One of the earliest archaeologists studying Greece's Stone Age was Christos Tsountas, who focused on Neolithic (Late Stone Age) materials from the Thessalian plain beginning in 1901. Adalbert Markovits excavated the Zaimis Cave in Attica and the Ulbricht Cave in the Argolid Peninsula in the 1920s. He identified artifacts dating to the Paleolithic (Early Stone Age) and Mesolithic (Middle Stone Age) eras.

Meanwhile, Gordon Childe explored Neolithic finds in the Thessalian plain, noticing a resemblance between Greek artifacts and those found in western Asia. He believed Thessaly's exceptionally developed Neolithic civilization was Europe's first example of settled villages and agriculture. Radiocarbon dating places Greek sites in Thessaly and in the Peloponnese of southern Greece to be slightly younger than western Asia's Neolithic sites. Greece is located at the crossroads of early human migrations, and recent evidence points to Greece as the hub of Europe's earliest Stone Age cultures.

In the 1960s, Eric Higgs of the University of Cambridge began an archaeological exploration of Epirus in northwestern Greece. He found artifacts establishing a Paleolithic civilization with continuous occupation over extended periods. In 1967, Thomas Jacobsen of Indiana University began excavating the Franchthi Cave overlooking the Argolic Gulf in southern Greece. The cave served as a seasonal shelter for Paleolithic-era hunters. The discovery of obsidian (a black volcanic stone) from the island of Melos in the Aegean Sea proved the people had seafaring technology in the Early Stone Age.

Mesolithic-era artifacts in the Franchthi Cave showed a transition from big-game hunting to fishing for tuna and harvesting wild plants. The Neolithic-era people in the Franchthi area carved figurines of people and animals and built stone houses and terraces for crops. In 2015, divers discovered an underwater city at Lambayanna Beach just around the bend from the cave. Its earliest layers date to the transitional era between the Neolithic and Bronze Ages. Rising sea waters buried the once-thriving city, which survived well into the Bronze Age, with fortification walls, high towers, and paved roads.[2]

Genetic studies indicate the Neolithic Greeks who practiced agriculture originated in western Turkey and spread from Greece throughout Europe.[3] The earliest Neolithic settlements in Greece did not have pottery, but they farmed, fished, and raised cattle, goats, sheep, and pigs. In the Argolid Peninsula and Thessaly, they lived in villages that consisted of up to one hundred people. They grew barley, lentils, peas, and wheat. Their tools and weaponry were made of obsidian and flint. Although they apparently sailed to Milos for its razor-sharp volcanic obsidian glass, no one lived on the island until the Late Neolithic era.

By 6000 BCE, the Neolithic Greeks had developed pottery-making, which they painted and fired in kilns. By 5000 BCE, they used stone foundations for houses, which had porches and several rooms. They lived in walled villages of up to three hundred people. They learned to carve stone and marble, producing small figurines of broad-shouldered, wide-hipped women, sometimes holding a baby. In addition to wheat, they grew rye and oats, which they used to bake bread in clay ovens. They wove garments from sheep wool. By 4000 BCE, their clay pottery featured arresting polychrome decorations.

Greece's earliest Bronze Age culture was the Minoans, who settled on Crete around 3500 BCE and later colonized other islands, including Rhodes and Thera. Crete is located in the Mediterranean Sea; it is almost halfway between mainland Greece and North Africa. The archaeologist Sir Arthur Evans named Crete's original civilization "Minoan" after Minos, who was identified by ancient historians as Crete's first king. According to Greek myth, Minos was the son of the god Zeus and a human mother, Europa, a Phoenician princess living in southern Greece. Zeus abducted her from Greece, brought her to Crete, and made

[2] Julien Beck, et al. "Searching for Neolithic Sites in the Bay of Kiladha, Greece," *Quaternary International* 584 (May 20, 2021):129-40.
https://www.sciencedirect.com/science/article/pii/S1040618220308466#!

[3] Hofmanová, Zuzana, et al. "Early Farmers from across Europe Directly Descended from Neolithic Aegeans." *PNAS.* 113 (25) (June 6, 2016): 6886–6891.
doi:10.1073/pnas.1523951113. ISSN 0027-8424. PMC 4922144. PMID 27274049.

her his queen. They had three children, with Minos being the oldest.

The Phoenicians were seafaring people centered in Lebanon. However, they conducted trade and established colonies throughout the Mediterranean, including southern Greece. The Minos myth may reflect the blending of Crete's Phoenician and Greek colonists. DNA sampling indicates that Crete was settled by people from the central Levant (today's Syria, Lebanon, and Israel) and later by Mycenean Greeks.[4]

Greek myth said that Minos angered the god of the sea, Poseidon, when the deity sent him a magnificent snow-white bull to signify he was destined to be king. Instead of sacrificing the bull to Poseidon, Minos kept it for himself and sacrificed a different bull. Poseidon retaliated by placing a spell on Minos's wife, Pasiphaë, who became enraptured with the bull and had sex with it. She gave birth to a monster: the half-man, half-bull Minotaur who devoured humans. Minos built a labyrinth to contain the horrific creature but had to find people to feed him.

After the Athenians killed his son, an enraged Minos sailed to Athens to avenge him. Minos's father, Zeus, punished the city with disease and starvation. To escape Zeus's wrath, Minos ordered the Athenians to send seven boys and seven girls every nine years to feed the Minotaur. Athens sent fourteen children to the monster two times. The hero Theseus accompanied the children the third time. He made his way through the labyrinth and killed the Minotaur.

Minos probably was a real person (minus the Minotaur). He ruled around 2000 BCE when the Minoan culture took a great leap forward. Before then, the Minoans had gradually been cultivating a civilization on Crete for 1,500 years. They developed trade centers and a class hierarchy on the island. Around 2000 BCE, they suddenly surged forward and became a complex civilization, establishing Europe's first palaces and cities.

---

[4] King, RJ, et al. "Differential Y-chromosome Anatolian Influences on the Greek and Cretan Neolithic." *Annals of Human Genetics*. 72 (March 2008):205-14. doi: 10.1111/j.1469-1809.2007.00414.x. PMID: 18269686.

The Minoan civilization's transformation may well have been due to visionary leadership. The historian Thucydides said Minos built Crete's first navy (probably the first navy anywhere), enabling the Minoans to become a great sea power in the Mediterranean. Minos took possession of the Cyclades island group north of Crete with his fleet. He fought Athens and ruled the Aegean and Mediterranean Seas. The Cretans traded with Egypt and western Asia, adopting some of their technology and art techniques.

This restored section reveals the splendor of the palace at Knossos.
cavorite *https://www.flickr.com/photos/cavorite/*, *CC BY-SA 2.0*
<*https://creativecommons.org/licenses/by-sa/2.0*>, *via Wikimedia Commons;*
https://commons.wikimedia.org/wiki/File:Palace_of_Knossos.jpg

The Minoans began building breathtaking palaces around 2000 BCE in Crete's cities of Knossos, Malia, Phaistos, and Zakros. Earthquakes destroyed the original palaces, so the people rebuilt them around 1700 BCE. The four-story palaces towered over the landscape. They had a central court, massive colonnades, dazzling frescos decorating the walls, and archive libraries containing Europe's first two written languages.

Artisans in the palace workshops produced enchanting figurines and pottery for trading throughout the Aegean and Mediterranean. These palaces served as regional centers of administration, religion, and trade for the surrounding farms and towns. A road network traveled outward from the palaces to nearby communities. The palaces stored grain, oil, and wine, perhaps for trade or as emergency provisions in the event of drought or other disasters.

Each palace was independent of the others during the first few centuries. After the palaces were rebuilt around 1700 BCE, Knossos rose to supremacy over the rest of the island. The palaces had no fortification walls, indicating the communities coexisted peacefully and did not fear foreign invasion. But they also had armor, bows and arrows, and swords. Perhaps this was for their naval attacks off the island. However, watchtowers on the roads between the palaces suggest bandits might have been a problem in remote areas of the island.

The Minoan civilization was remarkably advanced. The people created astounding architecture, lively artwork, aqueducts, sewage systems, and water treatment devices. The Minoans had Europe's first two writing systems (still undeciphered), which were found on seals and clay tablets. Their first writing system, used from 2100 to 1700 BCE, was Cretan hieroglyphs, which used stylized pictures to represent words or sounds. Egypt began using hieroglyphic writing around 3200 BCE, and the Minoans interacted and traded with Egypt. However, although they are superficially similar, the Cretan system was distinct. Egypt had over eight hundred symbols, while Cretan hieroglyphics only had eighty-five known symbols. Although it hasn't yet been decoded, the low number of symbols indicates that Cretan hieroglyphic was a phonetic script, with each symbol representing a sound.

The second writing system was Linear A, which came into use around 1800 BCE. It was probably a phonetic alphabet. It likely followed the same system as Cretan hieroglyphics but with simplified graphics. Linear A is unlike Egyptian hieroglyphics and Mesopotamian cuneiform, although it is possibly linked to the Proto-Sinaitic script, the ancestor of the Phoenician alphabet. Archaeologists have found hundreds of clay tablets inscribed with Linear A.

The Minoans produced high-quality ceramics, including delicately thin drinking vessels and vibrant pottery that initially featured geometric designs and later flowers and fish. Their art pictured men wearing loincloths and women in long gowns.

Women seemed to be socially equal to men. The dynamic Minoan artwork showed men, women, animals, and sea creatures in bold action.

Minoan buildings and artwork suggest their religious worship included feasts, parades, and offering food and drink to their deities. The bull was an essential feature of Minoan culture. The Minoans sacrificed bulls, and their walls, jewelry, and figurines depicted bulls more than any other animal. Minoan art shows the curious practice of bull leaping, where a man grabbed a bull by the horns and flipped himself over its back.

This fresco at the Palace at Knossos shows a man vaulting over a bull.
George Groutas, CC BY 2.0 <https://creativecommons.org/licenses/by/2.0>, via Wikimedia Commons;
https://commons.wikimedia.org/wiki/File:Bull_leaping,_fresco_from_the_Great_Palace_at_Knossos,_Crete,_Heraklion_Archaeological_Museum.jpg

An important deity was a goddess holding two snakes and wearing a long, tiered skirt. Female priestesses wearing long robes are also shown sacrificing bulls and other offerings. Worship took place in palaces, mountain peaks, and caves. Archaeological excavations revealed human sacrifices; in one case, an earthquake struck while the Minoans were sacrificing a teenage boy, crushing the boy's killers.[5] The Minoans at Knossos practiced child sacrifice and cannibalism, which may have given rise to the myth of sacrificing children to the Minotaur.[6]

The Minoan society violently collapsed due to a combination of natural disasters and invasion. The 1700 BCE earthquake destroyed most of Crete's urban centers, yet the Cretans were able to recover and rebuild. But about a century later, a volcano on the island of Thera erupted catastrophically. The VEI-7 magnitude of the monstrous Minoan eruption was like multiple atomic bombs exploding. It sent ten million tons of rock, ash, and gas twenty miles up, penetrating the stratosphere.

Two hundred feet of ash and pumice buried those who hadn't escaped Thera. The volcano and accompanying earthquakes triggered a disastrous tsunami that submerged Crete's northern coast, destroying its ports and many of its cities. Some of the Minoans on Crete survived the tsunami and earthquakes, and their civilization continued until 1100 BCE, although it was significantly weakened and vulnerable.

Meanwhile, the Myceneans were thriving in the southern Greece mainland. The Minoans had lost many ports and administrative centers, so they could not maintain their sovereignty over the Mediterranean. The Myceneans stepped into the void around 1450 BCE, replacing Minoan settlements with trade outposts of their own. It appears they also invaded Crete around 1420 BCE, burning all the remaining palaces except for Knossos, which the Myceneans renovated. Archaeological finds reveal a Mycenean presence coexisting with the Minoans in Crete until the Bronze Age Collapse.

---

[5] Rodney Castleden, *The Knossos Labyrinth: A New View of the 'Palace of Minos' at Knossos* (London: Routledge, 2012), 121-22.

[6] Peter Warren, "Knossos: New Excavations and Discoveries," *Archaeology* 37, no. 4 (1984): 48-55. http://www.jstor.org/stable/41731580

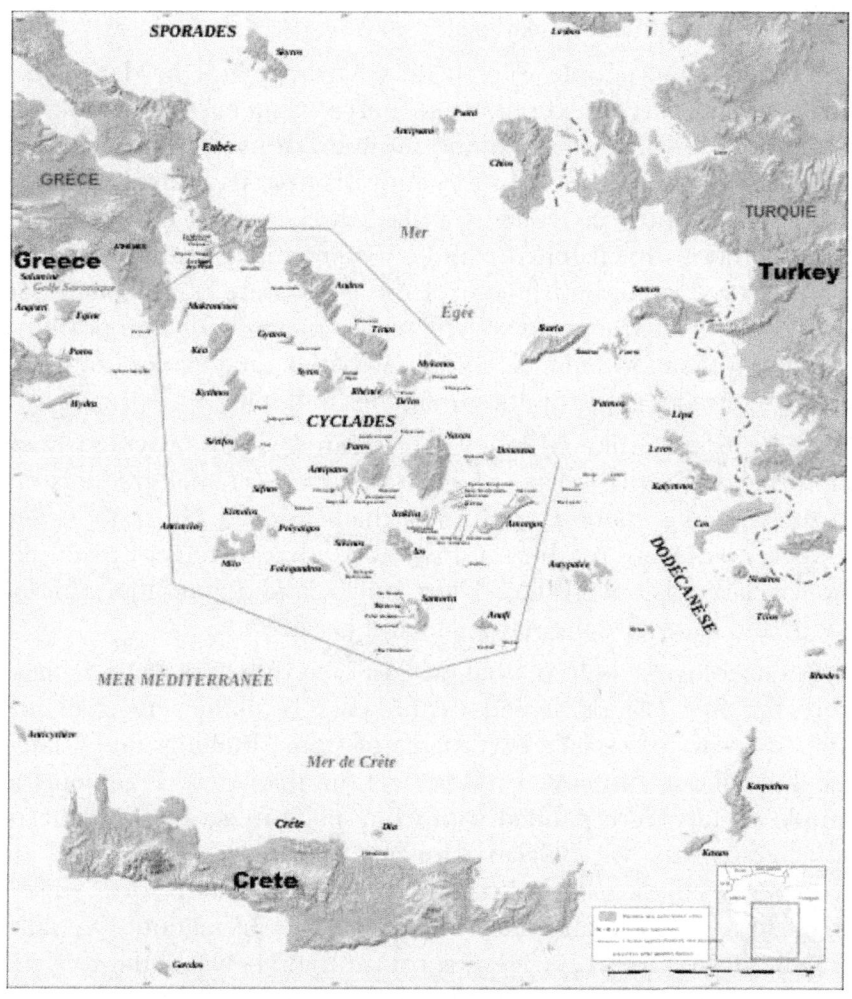

The Cyclades are between Greece and Turkey and north of Crete.
Credit: Eric Gaba (Sting - fr:Sting), CC BY-SA 3.0
<https://creativecommons.org/licenses/by-sa/3.0>, via Wikimedia Commons;
https://commons.wikimedia.org/wiki/File:Cyclades_map-fr.svg

The Cycladic civilization emerged around 3200 BCE. They were seafaring people on the Cyclades in the Aegean Sea. The word "Cyclades" means "encircling islands." This island group forms a roughly circular shape around the sacred island of Delos. Delos was a worship center and later became the mythical birthplace of the Greek deities Artemis and Apollo. The Cycladic civilization and the Minoans existed in the same timeframe. They were in close proximity to each other and interacted. The Minoans colonized some of the southern Cyclades.

The Cycladic people were fishers, farmers, and herders. Their small boats were susceptible to fierce winter storms, so they spearfished for tuna mainly in the summer, which was also when the fish came closer to shore. In the Late Bronze Age, they built larger and stronger ships propelled by fifty rowers, which enabled deep-sea expeditions for fishing or trade. Today, many of the islands are sparsely populated, and fifteen of the islands are uninhabited. But before deforestation and overgrazing, the islands supported a thriving population. The people grew barley, grapevines, and olive trees on terraces going up the mountains and hills.

Some islands, like Milos, were volcanic. They provided razor-sharp black obsidian glass, which was valued for making tools and weapons. Other mineral resources that enriched the islands were copper, gold, iron, marble, and silver. With a surplus of resources, the Cycladic people sailed from one island to another, trading goods and exporting them to mainland Greece.

Archaeologists believe that Mykonos, Antiparos, and Saliagos were the first islands settled in the Late Neolithic era. Neolithic ruins on Saliagos revealed remnants of stone dwellings and a larger building about fifty by forty-six feet in diameter. Fragments of simple pottery were painted with white paint in geometric patterns. The craftsmen of Saliagos formed obsidian spear tips and arrowheads in a narrow triangular or leaf-shaped form. These characteristic obsidian pieces were found throughout Neolithic settlements in Greece, suggesting robust trade between the Cyclades and the mainland.

Marble figurines, usually female, became a hallmark of Cycladic culture. They were typically about a foot high, but a few were almost life-sized. Some were violin-shaped, with unnaturally long heads and necks and sometimes no legs. Their faces often had no features other than a nose, although the eyes and mouth might have been painted. They were usually unearthed from the graves of men and women. Scholars debate whether they had religious significance.

This marble figurine is from the island of Naxos, circa 3000 BCE.
Zoomed in. Credit: Zde, CC BY-SA 3.0 <https://creativecommons.org/licenses/by-sa/3.0>,
via Wikimedia Commons;
https://commons.wikimedia.org/wiki/File:Cycladic_figurine_female,_3200%E2%80%9328
00_BC,_AshmoleanM,_AN_1946.118,_142402.jpg

Archaeologists have found forty graves on the island of Kea. The adult graves had walled crypts, each holding one to thirteen adults. Jars or tiny stone coffins held deceased children and babies. Crypt and stone coffin burials were also found on the islands of Amorgos and Syros. This burial style was far more advanced than mainland Greece in the same era, implying a distinct culture in the Cyclades.[7] A curious archaeological find in some graves in the Cyclades are hundreds of "frying pans": flat, round objects of decorated pottery or stone with a handle. Their purpose remains a mystery.

---

[7] John E. Coleman, "The Chronology and Interconnections of the Cycladic Islands in the Neolithic Period and the Early Bronze Age," *American Journal of Archaeology* 78, no. 4 (1974): 333–44. https://doi.org/10.2307/502747.

This Cycladic "frying pan" dates to about 2700 BCE.
© Marie-Lan Nguyen / Wikimedia Commons;

When the Minoan civilization on Crete rose to prominence around 2000 BCE, its sophisticated culture overshadowed the Cycladic civilization. The Minoans settled some of the southern Cyclades, and evidence shows a shared culture between Crete and the Cyclades. The tsunami and earthquakes accompanying the apocalyptic Minoan eruption in the southern Cyclades would have probably wiped out most life on the nearby islands. Yet, the Cycladic culture survived for several centuries until it collapsed around 1050 BCE. The Minoan culture had already disintegrated, followed by the Myceneans, as Greece fell into its centuries-long Dark Ages.

Chapter 2: The Mycenaeans and the Dark Ages

"My brother! Have you forgotten your oath?" King Menelaus of Sparta paced back and forth in agitation. Paris had abducted his wife Helen and taken her to Troy. He needed his brother, King Agamemnon of Mycenae, to help him get her back.

"Yes, Menelaus, I remember we all promised Helen's father to defend her marriage to whomever he chose. But I'm thinking of what it will take to attack Troy. It's a powerful city, and we will surely lose countless men if we go to war. We need to gather as many allies as possible if we hope to win. And if we achieve victory, it will bring us control of the Dardanelles. Greece will reap great power and wealth if we have free access to the straits and the Black Sea."

Once thought to be a myth, the prolonged and devastating Trojan War has recently found archaeological support. The "long-haired Achaeans," as Homer called the Mycenaeans, were laser-focused on controlling the trade routes of the Mediterranean, Aegean, and Black Seas. They willingly crushed their rivals, but in the end, they overextended themselves and brought down their own civilization.

Where did the Mycenaeans come from? Genetic analysis indicates they and the Minoans both descended from the ancient steppe herdsmen of today's Turkey, Armenia, and Iran. However, unlike the Minoans, the Mycenaean DNA was one-quarter linked to Siberia and northeastern Europe.[8] In the mid-Bronze Age, these Indo-European people swept into central and southern Greece, establishing the Mycenaean civilization. It thrived from 1750 to 1050 BCE, lifting the region to new heights of architecture, engineering, and military expertise.

How did the Myceneans become a great power in mainland Greece and beyond? By assimilating culture and expertise from the Minoans, the Myceneans developed a brilliantly advanced civilization. The militant Mycenaeans conquered Greece and Crete and grew wealthy through trade with the Cyclades, Cyprus, Egypt, and Phoenicia. Their ingenious engineers constructed stupendous fortresses, water and sewage systems, and bridges. The later Greek civilizations immortalized them with myths of their exploits and tales of heroes like Achilles and Odysseus.

The center of the Mycenaean civilization was the city of Mycenae in southern Greece's Peloponnese Peninsula. Mycenae was close to Athens and Corinth on a high hill just inland from the Saronic Gulf. Its limestone defensive walls are almost twenty feet thick and were constructed without mortar. Its stones are so huge that legend says the one-eyed Cyclops built the walls. Some of the walls are still standing today over three thousand years later. Mycenae's megaron (the great hall that contained the throne room) was supported by four columns with an elevated platform for the king.

[8] I. Lazaridis, et al. "Genetic Origins of the Minoans and Mycenaeans." *Nature* 548 (August 10, 2017): 214-18. doi: 10.1038/nature23310. Epub 2017 Aug 2. PMID: 28783727; PMCID: PMC5565772.

The Lion Gate still stands over three thousand years later.
William Neuheisel from DC, US, CC BY 2.0

The Lion Gate has ten-foot-high rectangular boulders at each side of the entrance supporting a twenty-ton lintel. Over the lintel is a carving of two lions. It was built around 1250 BCE and is a stunning engineering feat. It resembles a gate to the Hittite city of Hattusa; however, the Mycenae gate and walls are more refined, with boulders that fit together better. How was that gargantuan lintel raised to rest on the side jambs? Some theorize that megalithic structures like this one involved building a temporary earthen ramp up to the top, lugging the huge lintel up the ramp, perhaps on rollers, getting it into place, and then removing the ramp. It must have involved massive manpower. It's no wonder the Greeks thought the Cyclops built it!

The Myceneans built their palaces within a fortified citadel called an acropolis, which was usually located at the top of a hill. The archaic and classical Greeks continued to place their palaces and temples in a hilltop acropolis. The rest of the city would be spread out below, with the majestic palace and temple area towering above, surrounded by massive walls. The high location provided dual protection: the guardsmen could survey the entire surrounding area, and it was easier to defend from attacks. In the event of an attack, the regular citizens would hurry up the hill to take refuge within the walls.

Although more humble, Tiryns was older than Mycenae, according to Greek mythology and archaeological evidence. Overlooking the Argolic Gulf, it was ten miles south of Mycenae and served as a major port. The Myceneans built its citadel around 1600 BCE and its first palace a little over two centuries later. An earthquake destroyed the palace in 1200 BCE; however, the city continued to grow to a population of fifteen thousand by 1050 BCE. It was one of the few cities in Greece that survived the Dark Ages.

The best-preserved Mycenean palatial structure is the Palace of Nestor in Pylos, which Homer mentioned in the *Iliad* and the *Odyssey*. Located on the southwest Peloponnese Peninsula coast, its earliest settlement may date back to 2000 BCE. Large-scale construction of the city began in 1600 BCE; however, the palace and other structures on Pylos's acropolis burned down in 1400 BCE. The palace was rebuilt and stood for about two more centuries before it burned again in 1180.

Colorful frescos, some still preserved, decorated the palace walls. Clay tablets contained the most extensive Mycenean Linear B script collection on the Greek mainland. Once Linear B was decoded, these tablets provided valuable information about the Mycenean culture and political system. Other major Mycenean centers with palaces included Athens, Sparta, and Thebes, although over one hundred towns and cities dotted Greece's landscape.

This vivid fresco of a dove and lyre player decorated Pylos's palace wall.

The major Mycenean centers served as the political head of the states, with a king (*anax*) ruling from the palace and controlling the industries in the region. Each state was divided into districts and had a central city or town, which also had a palace or fortress. Tiryns was probably one of those "district towns" under Mycenae. All the states were in a confederation subject to a "great king," who likely ruled from Mycenae.[9]

The *anax* also served as a judge and military commander. The kings came from the warrior, landowning aristocracy. A council of elders served as advisors to the king, a system that continued in the archaic and classical eras. The Myceneans had three basic social classes: the military aristocracy, the regular people (farmers, craftsmen, merchants, etc.), and enslaved people who served in the palace and temples.

---

[9]Jorrit M. Kelder, *The Kingdom of Mycenae: A Great Kingdom in the Late Bronze Age Aegean* (Bethesda: CDL Press, 2010), 45, 86, 106-7.

The Mycenean economy centered around trade. Their ships sailed as far as Spain in the west and into the Black Sea in the east. Defeating Troy meant gaining control of the Dardanelles, which connected the Aegean and Black Seas. The Myceneans established colonies around the Mediterranean and Aegean Seas to support their trade networks. They exported olives, olive oil, raisins, pottery, linen and wool textiles, and wine. They imported copper, tin, and luxury goods.

Mycenean art reflected Minoan influences, but the Myceneans put their own stamp on it. They worked with larger pieces than the Minoans, embraced new materials to work with, and used novel styles like abstract imagery. They were known for their eye-catching pottery and frescos that focused on themes of war, religion, hunting, and nature, especially sea life. The palace workshops produced glass articles, finely cut gems, and vases made from precious metals.

The Myceneans developed the Minoan's Linear A script into Linear B. They used a similar form as Linear A, although they included a few new signs. The significant difference was the two writing systems represented different languages. The Minoan language has been extinct for over two millennia, and we still don't know what sort of language it was. When archaeologists began unearthing all the clay tablets at Pylos, no one could read Linear B, but in 1952, Michael Ventris cracked the code.

Ventris was an architect but had developed a keen interest in Linear B as a teenager. As an adult, he continued trying to decipher the language. By observing patterns, he determined that Linear B had eighty-nine characters. That meant it was mostly a phonetic script, with signs representing sounds rather than whole words, although it also had over one hundred non-phonetic ideograms. Ventris eventually realized the Mycenean language was an ancient form of Greek.

When the Myceneans began building palaces, they also built shrines close to or within the citadels. The administrative centers also acted as religious centers. The palatial structures in Pyros and Mycenae contained altars in their courtyard or porch. Like the Minoans, the Myceneans sacrificed bulls in their religious observances and poured out water in libation. Mycenae's temple contained multiple figurines of what appear to be worshipers and deities, along with fifteen clay snakes.

Frescos in the temple show several women who were either goddesses or priestesses. Linear B clay tablets list sacrifices of grain, honey, scented oil, and spices. The Myceneans were polytheistic, worshiping some of the same gods as later classical Greeks, including Zeus (called Diktaios on Crete), Ares (A-re), Artemis (A-te-mi-to), Dionysus (Di-wo-nu-so), Hera (E-ra), Hermes (E-ma), and their chief deity Poseidon (Po-se-da-o). They had a powerful female deity called Potnia (mistress), possibly Athena's equivalent, and female versions of Zeus and Poseidon (Diwia and Posidaia), who were not worshiped in later Greek eras.[10]

Like the Cycladic civilization and the Minoans, the Myceneans often buried their dead in coffins, but instead of making them from stone, they usually made them from decorated clay. Shaft tombs in a circle are just outside the Lion Gate at the Palace of Nestor; the aristocrats of Pylos were buried there. The Mycenean shaft tombs were up to twelve feet deep. They were rectangular-shaped, with pebble floors and masonry walls. A wooden plank roof covered each grave. On top of that were an earthen mound and a stele or tombstone. Each shaft tomb held two to five bodies. Gold jewelry, cups, and death masks were buried with the occupants, while warriors were buried with their weapons. After scouring the writings of Homer and the 2nd-century CE Greek geographer Pausanias for clues, the amateur archaeologist Heinrich Schliemann discovered the shaft tombs in 1876.

---

[10] Susan Lupack, "Mycenaean Religion," in *The Oxford Handbook of the Bronze Age Aegean*, ed. Eric H. Cline, (2012). 10.1093/oxfordhb/9780199873609.013.0020.

The Myceneans put death masks over the faces of important people. This mask found by Schliemann at Mycenae dates to about 1550 BCE.

National Archaeological Museum of Athens, CC BY 2.0
<https://creativecommons.org/licenses/by/2.0>, via Wikimedia Commons;
https://commons.wikimedia.org/wiki/File:MaskOfAgamemnon.jpg

In the *Iliad*, Homer says that King Agamemnon of Mycenae led a coalition of Greek forces across the Aegean Sea to the city of Troy. The purported reason for the invasion was retrieving Menelaus's wife, Helen, from Prince Paris. However, the potential of controlling the passage from the Aegean to the Black Sea no doubt enabled Agamemnon to recruit Greek allies. After ten years of war, the Myceneans finally overpowered and burned down Troy by gaining entry via the Trojan Horse. King Menelaus got Helen back, and the Greek heroes sailed home.

Historians mostly dismissed the Trojan War as pure myth, but the ancient Greeks believed it was an actual historical event that happened around 1200 BCE. They said Troy was in today's northwestern Turkey at the entrance to the Dardanelles. In 1870, Heinrich Schliemann, the same amateur archaeologist who later discovered the graves at Pylos, traveled to Turkey. He met with Charles Maclaren and Frank Calvert, who believed that a low hill on a flat plain could be ancient Troy. Schliemann dug a deep trench from the center of the hill down to the bottom, revealing multiple layers of civilization.

Homer said an alternate name for Troy was the Hittite name Wilusa. He said that Prince Paris was also called Alaksandu. Hittite records say Wilusa was part of the Hittite Empire. It grew wealthy due to its strategic location for sea trade between the Black and Aegean Seas. Hittite documents said that Wilusa fought the "Ahhiyawa" and mentioned Alaksandu. Many scholars believe the Ahhiyawa were the Mycenaean Greeks.

Schliemann's excavation revealed nine layers of a powerful and wealthy city, with the oldest layer dating back to 3000 BCE. He found a layer dating from 1300 to 1180 BCE, with a domed citadel and other structures that matched Homer's description of Troy. This layer had evidence of a sudden catastrophic end about 1180 BCE: approximately when the ancient Greek historians said Troy fell.

Although the evidence isn't absolutely conclusive, the Myceneans may have destroyed Troy around 1180 BCE. But right about that same time, their civilization descended into chaos. Homer's *Odysseus* offers some clues for their collapse. If the Trojan War had really happened, the Greek kings and other key leaders would have been away from their realms for a decade. When they finally returned, they probably found destabilized states suffering from a lack of leadership.

With many of the warriors away, the cities were vulnerable to attack. The kings may have had to reassert their positions with whoever served as regent in their absence. King Agamemnon's wife took a lover in his absence, and when he returned home, she and her lover murdered him. Then, her son killed her and her lover to avenge Agamemnon's death. The Greeks and Trojans suffered horrific losses in the war. Many Greek cities lost their kings and countless warriors. The lives lost, the fortune expended on the war, and the destabilization it caused back in Greece may have led to an implosion of the Mycenean civilization.

But the Myceneans were not the only civilization to dissolve around 1200 BCE. From 1200 to 900 BCE, the Bronze Age Collapse saw the cataclysmic fall of numerous cultures in eastern Mediterranean regions: the Middle East, North Africa, and the Balkan Peninsula. Environmental catastrophes, including drought and earthquakes, weakened the region's societies. The mysterious marauding "Sea People" wreaked havoc on the coastal cities, from Egypt to Turkey. They shattered naval trade, cutting the Mediterranean supply chain and causing the system to collapse.

Most Mycenean cities lay in ashes, crumbling into oblivion after a destructive power crushed their majestic palaces. The Minoan and Cycladic civilizations likewise collapsed. The apocalypse was so abrupt and total that the Greek survivors lost their written languages, even in the few cities or towns that weren't demolished. Archaeologists have found no evidence of writing for three centuries in Greece.

Could the Sea People have been the Dorian Greeks? Greek legend said they had been exiled from Greece in the days of Heracles but returned from the north and took over the Peloponnese Peninsula in southern Greece. The Greek language had several dialects, and this seems to explain why. However, no definitive archaeological evidence has yet emerged to support a Dorian invasion. Cities were burned down, but new ones weren't built. Nothing innovative happened in Greece until about 1000 BCE when iron smelting slowly emerged.

The cause of the Greek Dark Ages remains a mystery. Perhaps it was a massive internal uprising or a pandemic. Large swathes of the population suddenly died, Greece's refined civilization melted away, and its economy dissipated. All the advances made by the Minoan and Mycenean civilizations were reversed. The reduced population continued farming, fishing, and herding but only to feed themselves in their small, impoverished communities. Greece's obscure Dark Ages continued for over three hundred years.

Greece slowly began emerging from the ashes of its shattered society around 800 BCE. This cultural renewal was based on the Mycenean past but was much simpler. The fluid and realistic scenes on Mycenean pottery gave way to abstract scenes and geometric patterns. The population began to increase again, building new cities or rebuilding old ones and erecting temples. Trade revived, and their economy began growing.

One technological advancement that marked the Dark Ages was the smelting of iron for tools and weapons, which transitioned Greece from the Bronze Age to the Early Iron Age. In the Bronze Age, Egypt and Mesopotamia produced small amounts of iron implements by hammering down meteorites, which are iron-nickel alloys. They didn't require smelting, but obviously, there weren't a lot of available meteorites.

Iron smelting emerged in Anatolia (Turkey) in the Bronze Age. Greece seemed to be on the brink of using this technology right before the Dark Ages, as archaeologists have found several iron tools or weapons dating from 1300 to 1200 BCE. The number of iron implements increased significantly around 1000 BCE, indicating the Greeks had mastered iron smelting in high-heat furnaces.

The Greeks began writing again around 770 BCE but not with Linear A or B. This time, they used the Semitic Phoenician alphabet as a guide but included vowels and adapted it to fit spoken Greek, which had different sounds. Over half of the letters of the ancient Greek alphabet are in today's western European alphabets, including English. Once the Greeks had a writing system again, they began using it in much broader applications than in the past. Linear B was mainly used for record-keeping, but the new Greek alphabet was used to write down the *Iliad* and the *Odyssey*. The new alphabet marked the transition to the archaic period, with its epic poetry and brilliant and prosperous civilization.

PART TWO:
From the Archaic Years to Roman Conquest (750–146 BCE)

Chapter 3: The Archaic Years

"Sire! I beg you! Don't sail your navy into the Bay of Eleusis. We will be at a disadvantage in the straits of Salamis. The Greeks' best naval maneuvers are in narrow waterways."

Queen Artemisia of Halicarnassus was one of King Xerxes I's naval commanders. He had led his million-man Persian force into Greece without resistance from the northern and central states. But southern Greece, led by Athens, Sparta, and Corinth, was the holdout.

"Artemisia, we've got them trapped! If we take Salamis, we can wipe out the Athenians. They're fighting each other right now. They're demoralized. This will be an easy win!"

Xerxes climbed Mount Aigaleo for the best view of his anticipated victory. Only a few Corinthian ships were floating in the bay. He couldn't see the three hundred Greek triremes hidden in the coves of Georgios Island. His self-assurance morphed into horror as he watched the debacle unfold. When his ships chased the Corinthian vessels into the straits, the Greek triremes moved in behind them, trapping the Persians in the narrow confines. Over and over, they rammed the Persian vessels until sinking ships and floating bodies clogged the water.

Greece's epic win against the massive Persian forces in 480 BCE was the defining moment in the Greco-Persian wars. From this point on, the Greeks were the aggressors, and the Persians were on the defense. It also marked the end of the archaic era, which began with the first Olympic Games in 776 BCE. Like the legendary phoenix, Greece arose from the Dark Ages more resilient and resplendent than ever. Greece's archaic era showcased enchanting poetry, novel philosophy, entrancing architecture and sculptures, and sensational advances in engineering, mathematics, and science.

Greece's Olympic sprinters on a 6ᵗʰ-century BCE amphora jar, with the newly introduced Greek letters above the runners.
RickyBennison, CC0, via Wikimedia Commons;
https://commons.wikimedia.org/wiki/File:Panathenaic_Amphora_Sprinters.jpg

The city of Olympia in the Peloponnese hosted the first Olympic Games as a festival for Zeus, which became a tradition every four years. Although the Greek city-states often battled each other, they formed a truce during the Olympics, guaranteeing safety at the games and while traveling to and from the contests. Athletes from a dozen cities came to the first Olympics for foot races. By the end of the archaic era, athletes came from one hundred cities in Greece and its colonies stretching from the Black Sea to the western Mediterranean. By this time, the competitions included chariot races, discus and javelin throws, the long jump, and military arts.

Ancient Greece was never one united country as it is today. Instead, it was a collection of independent city-states called *poleis* (singular *polis*) in mainland Greece and colonies around the

Aegean, Black, and Mediterranean Seas. A city-state consisted of a primary city with its surrounding farmland, villages, and towns. Toward the end of the archaic era, as some cities embraced democracy, the word polis meant the citizens of a city-state.

The city-states were politically independent of the others, with a variety of political structures. Some had kings, usually with an advisory council. Sparta had two kings. A small group of aristocrats called an oligarchy ruled some city-states. In Corinth, the men in their oligarchy were all from the same family. Later, tyrants ruled Corinth and some other cities. Athens went through the whole gamut during the archaic era: a monarchy, oligarchy, tyranny, and democracy.

Each polis was like its own small country, operating independently of the others, although they joined forces against a common enemy. Often, the common enemy was another Greek city-state. The most powerful and renowned cities in the archaic era were Sparta, Athens, Thebes, Corinth, Argos, Eretria, and Elis. They shared a common language, albeit with different dialects. They also shared the same polytheistic religion, with Zeus acting as the chief god. Each city-state had a patron deity. Poseidon was Corinth's patron, Dionysus was Thebe's divine patron, and Zeus's wife Hera was the head goddess of Argos.

Throughout the archaic era, Athens and Sparta were archrivals. Both were in southern Greece, only about 150 miles apart, but they were polar opposites in their philosophy, politics, lifestyle, and social structure. The Spartans were known for their rigid discipline and resistance to change. The Athenians were progressive and loved nothing better than debating the latest philosophies and ideas.

Sparta's two kings ruled with a council of elderly men who had retired from military service at the age of sixty. Sparta's lifestyle revolved around its military. Every able-bodied Spartan male citizen between the ages of twenty to sixty served in the military. Although the men married around the age of twenty, they lived in the barracks until they were thirty, making clandestine night visits to their wives. With their husbands away so much, the independent Spartan women conducted business affairs, wore short skirts, and learned martial skills.

While the rest of Greece was awakening from the Dark Ages, Sparta was in a state of anarchy. The Spartans finally pulled through with a series of reforms that set their society apart from the rest of Greece. Because all the men served in the military full-time, they needed someone to work the fields, so they conquered the neighboring Messenian and Laconian regions. They forced these people to be helots or serf laborers. The helots tended the fields. With every Spartan man freed up to serve full-time in the military, Sparta became Greece's most formidable military power by the end of the archaic era.

Athens had been a prominent Mycenean center, one of the few Greek cities to survive through the Dark Ages. Its ideal location for sea trade enabled Athens to thrive toward the end of the Dark Ages, helping to lift the rest of Greece out of inertia. Athens gained control of most of the Attica Peninsula in southern Greece, making it one immense city-state. It was the wealthiest and strongest state in the early archaic period.

While Sparta held to the same political and social structure throughout the archaic period, Athens underwent a series of changes. It had been a monarchy with a council in its Mycenean days and in the early archaic era. Then, it segued to a system of three primary magistrates called *archontes* leading the city-state. The *ecclesia* (male citizens' assembly) elected them from the elite class originally for life, then for ten-year terms, and finally for one year. One *archon* headed up the military, another led religious functions, and the third, the chief magistrate, was the administrative leader holding most of the power. Six other archons, called *thesmotetai*, served as judges.

By 621 BCE, the Athenians were increasingly unhappy with their unwritten laws, which led to confusion and exploitation. They asked Draco, Athens's first legislator, to write a law code. But Draco's laws were ridiculously harsh, mandating the death sentence for minor infractions. On the positive side, all Athenians, whether aristocrats or working class, had equal rights under Draco's legal system.

Twenty-seven years later, the Athenians asked their chief magistrate, Solon, to write a constitution. He rewrote Draco's laws and restructured the political system so males from all classes had voting rights. In his system, Athens had four classes, and each class had one hundred men appointed to the four-hundred-man council (called a *boule*). Not every citizen could vote, but one hundred voters equally represented each layer of society. It was a giant step toward democracy.

Athens's next step in its political journey was the rule of tyrants, which didn't necessarily mean a cruel despot. A tyrant came into power outside the usual channels. Instead of being the crown prince or elected by the ecclesia, he usually usurped the throne, sometimes through the assistance of oppressed citizens wanting a change. He had complete authority. He might have had an advisory council, but he had the ultimate say. As a usurper, he often ignored parts of the state's constitution, although he would generally keep most systems in place.

Although tyrants had absolute power, they sometimes used it to benefit their city-state, especially the poor and working classes. Archaic-era Greeks didn't consider tyrants bad or good; it depended on the man and his actions. Tyrants often manipulated their way into power when the current ruling powers ignored the needs of the masses. Tyrants curried the favor of the neglected and oppressed classes, promising reforms in exchange for support. But once a tyrant came into power, he had to follow through on his promises or risk losing his position. Tyranny was a stepping stone for archaic Greece between rule by a king or oligarchy to a rudimentary democracy.

Athens's first tyrant was the war hero General Pisistratus, a relative of Solon. When class conflict rocked Athens, Pisistratus portrayed himself as a champion of the lower classes, which constituted the majority of the city's population. Once in power, Pisistratus improved life for the working class and the oppressed poor. He gave farmers their lands back that had been seized due to debt and helped them develop more profitable farming with cash crops. He used his own wealth from his Macedonian gold mines to upgrade Athens's infrastructure and promoted festivals and games, which pleased all the classes. He improved Athens's navy and developed the entire Attica Peninsula into a productive and prosperous place. Athens fared so well under Pisistratus that other Greek city-states considered tyranny a viable option.

Pisistratus's son, Hippias, was Athens's next tyrant. He initially followed in his benevolent father's footsteps but then deteriorated to the point that Sparta invaded and installed Isagoras as the next chief magistrate. Isagoras exiled anyone he considered a political threat and seized their land. Finally, in 508 BCE, the Athenians revolted, expelled Isagoras, and made Cleisthenes, a democratic visionary, the next leader of Athens.

Cleisthenes's novel democratic reforms divided Athens and the rest of the Attica Peninsula into ten tribes. Each tribe had thirty units: ten from Athens, ten from the rural farmlands, and ten from the coastal region. Fifty male citizens from each of the ten tribes served on a five-hundred-man council for one year. All citizens—rich or poor, rural or urban—were equally represented, which was another significant step toward democracy. It still didn't give every citizen the right to vote, nor did it give women any representation. Still, it established a new political system that persisted into the classical age.

Perpetual warfare marked Greece's archaic age. The city-states often fought each other, but they also vied with Carthage in North Africa for control over trade and colonies around the Mediterranean. This conflict eventually erupted into the Punic Wars. The massive Persian Achaemenid Empire also warred against Greece beginning in 547 BCE, when Cyrus the Great conquered the Ionian Greek colonies on the eastern Aegean coastline. Darius the Great invaded Greece's mainland, a venture that ended in a humiliating defeat for the Persians at the Battle of Marathon in 490 BCE. Darius's son, Xerxes I, invaded Greece again in 480 BCE with his million-man army, another fiasco for Persia.

A 5th-century hoplite with his helmet behind him.
Jona Lendering, CC0, via Wikimedia Commons;
https://commons.wikimedia.org/wiki/File:Hoplite_5th_century.jpg

Two reasons for Greece's success in warfare were its stellar navy and almost indomitable phalanx formation in land battles. The Greek hoplite warriors wore bronze helmets covering their faces, along with bronze breastplates and shin guards. They carried bronze shields in their left hands and seven-foot spears in their right. They lined up in the phalanx position: shoulder to shoulder, with their shields slightly overlapping. Behind the first row of hoplites would be at least seven more rows. The phalanx was somewhat like a human bulldozer, approaching the enemy lines with long spears and a massive shield wall that crushed anyone not impaled by the spears.

The seafaring Greeks developed a fearsome navy in the archaic era that enabled them to fend off the Persian Empire. Their primary warship was the 120-foot-long trireme, which was propelled by rowers and sails. The ships had battering rams on their bows, and the Greeks were exceptionally skilled in ramming enemy ships in naval battles or swooping along the sides of their ships and shattering their oars. Their marine maneuvers, especially in straits or rivers, brought them a victory against Persia.

Although fierce warriors, the Greeks were also poets. Homer's epic poems, the *Iliad* and the *Odyssey*, were probably oral tales until they were finally written down with Greece's new alphabet. Hesiod wrote *Theogony* and *Works and Days* about creation and early human history. Hesiod chronicled the Golden Age when men did not sin and never knew hard labor or sadness. In the Silver Age, people had to work hard but lived long lives. The violent Bronze Age followed, which ended when Zeus wiped out the human race with the Great Flood. But Zeus told Deucalion, a man of integrity, to build an ark and fill it with food. Deucalion's family survived and formed Greece's three major tribes: the Aeolians, Dorians, and Achaeans.

Lyric poetry, sung to the lyre, became popular in the archaic age. Sappho of Lesbos wrote about love and desire between women. Mimnermus of Smyrna wrote war poetry about the Lydian Empire's invasion of his city. A choir sang and danced to choral lyric poetry, which was popular in Sparta; two favorite composers were Terpander of Lesbos and Alcman.

Corinth's Temple of Apollo, circa 540 BCE, displays Doric pillars.
Carole Raddato from FRANKFURT, Germany, CC BY-SA 2.0
<https://creativecommons.org/licenses/by-sa/2.0>, via Wikimedia Commons;
https://commons.wikimedia.org/wiki/File:Temple_of_Apollo,_built_ca._540_BC,_Corinth_, Greece_(14109129322).jpg

A hallmark sculpture style of the archaic era was life-sized marble or limestone *korai* and *kouroi* statues of slightly smiling young women and men. The women (korai) wore long braids and modest gowns, while the men (kouroi) were naked; both represented idealized youths. The Greeks built the first stone temples in the archaic age, following similar styles of wood and brick Mycenean palaces and temples. The earliest temple architecture was Doric, with pillars bulging out in the middle and friezes decorating the top.

The pre-Socratic philosophers shaped archaic Greece's spiritual, political, and intellectual understanding. Thales of Miletus is called the Father of Science; he sought scientific answers to why and how things happened rather than the common assumption that the gods controlled everything. Thales introduced geometric concepts to Greece, such as the diameter of a circle and that an isosceles triangle has equal base angles.

One of Thales's students was Anaximander, who taught that the god Atlas wasn't holding the world up; it naturally floated free. He maintained that nature followed specific laws, which must be respected. He once correctly predicted that an earthquake would hit Sparta and got the people evacuated to safety in time. One of Anaximander's students was Anaximenes, who figured out that stars and planets differed from each other. He perceived that stars move on the same planes in the same relative positions. However, the planets that he could observe with the naked eye had more complex movements.

Pythagoras had a school in the Greek colony of Samos in southern Italy. He proposed the novel concept that the earth was a sphere rather than flat. He worked out the Pythagorean theorem: the longest side squared of a ninety-degree triangle equals the sum of the other two sides squared ($a^2 + b^2 = c^2$). However, recent evidence shows that the Babylonians used the Pythagorean theorem about one thousand years before Pythagoras.[11]

Heraclitus of Ephesus taught that an unseen force called the Logos maintained and ran the universe. Humans must be in tune with the Logos to live correctly; however, most people try to live independently of the Logos and deceive themselves, failing to perceive actual reality. Xenophanes of Colophon laughed at the Greek deities who were no better than humans with their adultery, deceit, and conflict. He believed in an innately moral and benevolent supreme god who was above all gods and men.

As Greece woke up from the Dark Ages and began to prosper, its population quickly grew. But this created a problem because only 20 percent of Greece's rugged terrain could be farmed. The weather didn't help. Most of Greece's precipitation is in the winter, receiving hardly any rain during the growing season. The olive and fruit trees usually did well, but drought regularly ruined the grain crops.

Greece needed to thin out its mainland population, find a grain source to feed its people, and develop trade opportunities. The answer was colonization. During the first two centuries of the archaic era, the Greek city-states established five hundred colonies around the Mediterranean, Aegean, and Black Seas. Greek colonies

---

[11] D. F. Mansfield, "Plimpton 322: A Study of Rectangles," *Foundations of Science* 26 (2021): 977–1005. https://doi.org/10.1007/s10699-021-09806-0

extended west to today's Spain and France, south to North Africa, and as far northeast as today's Ukraine. Forty percent of the Greek population lived in its colonies, which were independent, self-governing states.

The hundreds of colonies on three continents brought unimaginable resources to Greece. The Greeks received not only grain but also lumber, textiles, and metals like copper, gold, iron, and tin. In return, Greece exported its famous red and black ceramics with scenes depicting battles, mythological scenes, and lively animals. Some of the exported pottery contained olives, olive oil, and wine from the Greece mainland. The colonies grew wealthy from trade, and some became centers for the arts or scholarly studies in mathematics, science, and philosophy.

Greece's vast trade system introduced it to coinage, which was invented in Lydia in the late 7th century BCE. Greece's first minted coins came from Aegina in the Saronic Gulf. Most ancient Greek coins were silver, but they also used gold, copper, and bronze. The city-states usually produced designs representing their city. Many used their patron deity, and the island of Thera had dolphins.

The archaic era was a high-energy age of unprecedented growth in population, colonization, technology, and scientific understanding. Archaic Greece made great strides in politics and culture. Its city-states developed formidable armies and navies that successfully allied to defeat the mammoth Persian Empire in two epic invasions. The archaic era set the stage for classical Greece's Golden Age.

Chapter 4: Classical Greece

"Are they insane? Do these Greeks think they have a chance against my million-man army?"

The year was 480 BCE, and Xerxes I of the Achaemenid Empire was swooping through Greece on his way to flatten Athens. But blocking his way in the narrow Thermopylae Pass was a small force of seven thousand Greek warriors led by King Leonidas of Sparta.

"You've got one last chance, Greeks! Throw down your weapons!"

The unfazed Spartans held their rigid discipline. "Come and get them!"

With their overlapping shields forming a wall in the phalanx position, the Greek allies held the line for two days. The pass was narrow, only sixteen feet from Mount Kallidromo's cliffs to the Malian Gulf. Behind the first line, the rest of the army stood resolute, ready to step into place if a soldier on the front line fell. But a fellow Greek eventually betrayed them, hoping for riches from Xerxes. He showed the Persians an alternate route through the mountains.

Realizing they were outflanked, King Leonidas sent most of the coalition army south, keeping only 1,400 soldiers in the pass. The joint forces heading south would guard the new wall at the Isthmus of Corinth, protecting Sparta, Corinth, and the rest of the

Peloponnese Peninsula. The remaining soldiers with Leonidas fought to the death, slowing the Persians' relentless march south.

Three major military confrontations rocked Greek's classical age, which lasted from 480 to 356 BCE: the last days of the Greco-Persian Wars, the Peloponnesian War, and a fierce conflict between Sparta and Thebes. The classical age is also renowned for its temples with stunning architecture, fluid and dynamic sculptures, enlightening philosophy, and groundbreaking concepts in mathematics and science.

King Leonidas's sacrifice at the Battle of Thermopylae gave the Athenians time to flee their city and regroup on the island of Salamis. Athens fell to Xerxes, but the Persians' humiliating loss in the naval Battle of Salamis convinced Xerxes to return to Persia for good. The Greeks realized their phenomenal victory against Persia was due to the allied city-states' joint forces. To eliminate the Persian threat once and for all, the Greeks formed the Delian League in 478 BCE.

Athens was in charge of the league, and the Greeks drove the Persians out of the Aegean Sea for fifteen years and chased off the Dolopian pirates disrupting Greek trade. However, an attempt to assist Egypt's revolt against Persian domination in 460 BCE ended in disaster: Athens lost much of its fleet and twenty thousand soldiers. Unnerved, General Pericles decided to move the Delian League's treasury to Athens, fearing it was vulnerable to the Persians at Delos. However, by controlling the league and now holding its treasury, Athens became a de facto empire, and contributions to the Delian League's treasury became tribute payments.

The final face-off between Persia and Greece occurred in 451 BCE over control of the island of Cyprus. Athens's General Cimon sailed two hundred ships to Cyprus, crushing the Persian fleet and forcing Persia to agree to the thirty-year Peace of Callias in 449 BCE. The Greek colonies in Asia won independence, and Persia promised to stay out of the Aegean Sea. Greece agreed not to interfere in Cyprus, Egypt, and Anatolia (today's western Turkey).

Athens was now reveling in its golden age. The period of peace enabled it to surge ahead economically and leave a breathtaking legacy in the sciences and culture. Democracy flowered under General Pericles's leadership, as he reformed its constitution and opened civil service positions to all social classes. He even paid the lower classes for jury service and other public administrative functions.

The remains of the Parthenon still crown Athens's Acropolis.

Athens had matured into the intellectual and artistic center of the Mediterranean. Xerxes had flattened Athens in 480 BCE, but Pericles rebuilt the citadel walls and temples on the Acropolis, which towered over the city. The Parthenon was the goddess Athena's elegant temple. A forty-foot image of the deity stood in the central room, surrounded by wall panels depicting mythological creatures and the Trojan War. The Propylaea is a colossal marble gate with Doric pillars standing in front of another image of Athena, this one made of bronze. Ictinus, the architect of Athens's Parthenon, also built the Temple of Apollo in the city of Bassae in the Peloponnese, combining Corinthian, Doric, and Ionic architecture.

Greece's Golden Age is legendary for its flowing and lively sculptures, capturing movement and emotion. The marble sculpture of *Hermes of Praxiteles* holding the baby Dionysus illustrates the relaxed contrapposto pose typical in the classical era, with the weight shifted to one leg. The classical Greeks preferred to use lustrous bronze for sculptures because of its strength, but the Romans later copied many Greek sculptures in marble.

This sculpture of Hermes and baby Dionysus was in Olympia's Temple of Hera.
Paolo Villa, CC BY-SA 4.0 <https://creativecommons.org/licenses/by-sa/4.0>, via Wikimedia Commons;
https://commons.wikimedia.org/wiki/File:02_2020_Grecia_photo_Paolo_Villa_FO190025_(Museo_archeologico_di_Olimpia_-_Statua_Ermes_con_Dioniso_Bambino_scolpita_da_Prassitele,_Arte_pre_Ellenistica,_det_taglio_superiore).jpg

A favorite recreational pastime for Greeks in the Golden Age was dramatic performances, sometimes comedies but more often tragedies. The themes focused on the gods meddling in human affairs and the implications of immorality, hopeless love, and treachery. Aeschylus, Euripides, and Sophocles were the most well-known playwrights. One of Euripides's tragedies portrayed Helen's version of why she left her husband for Prince Paris of Troy. Sophocles' *Oedipus Rex* tells the story of how King Laius wanted to kill his infant son because of a prophecy that said his son would kill him. But instead of his wife, Jocasta, killing her baby, she abandoned him. A shepherd found the infant, whom the king of Corinth adopted. When the child Oedipus grew up, he killed his biological father and married his mother without knowing their true identities.

Classical Greece made incredible strides in medicine, mathematics, science, and philosophy. Hippocrates, the "Father of Medicine," introduced clinical diagnosis: checking one's pulse, temperature, urine, and bowel movements and investigating pain level and range of motion. Theaetetus of Athens advanced geometry by developing Platonic solids and irrational lengths. Leucippus and his student Democritus developed a theory of atoms as the building blocks of matter. They correctly believed atoms were constantly in motion, which Leucippus said wasn't random but controlled by Logos (the unseen force that runs the world).

Hippias of Elis was a philosopher who delved into the realms of astronomy, mathematics, and music. He discovered the geometric quadratrix, a curve trisecting an angle. He believed that a fixed and universal natural law determined morality and that it was unchanging in all situations and eras. For instance, he taught that honoring one's parents was a natural law that persisted through time.

The philosopher Socrates used a question-and-answer teaching method, encouraging his students to come to their own conclusions rather than being fed knowledge. He said an unexamined life is not worth living; we need to understand the depths of what we do not know and constantly learn new things about ourselves and life. He said people who never questioned the status quo or asked questions were "double fools." They were fools for not knowing anything and double fools for not realizing their ignorance.

Socrates's challenges to his students resulted in his trial for the corruption of Athens's youth. He was also tried for impiety because he said his god was morally good and rational. He scorned the Greek gods, who lied and cheated on their spouses. Socrates asked how humans could be moral if their gods weren't. He was found guilty on both counts and sentenced to death by drinking hemlock.

Painting by Jacques-Louis David of Socrates's execution.

Socrates's student and close friend Plato taught the theory of forms, which stated that our concept of reality is only a reflection of actual reality. He said it is as if we live in a cave seeing shadows cast by the sun. We think the shadows are reality, but the true reality is the sun outside the cave, whose radiance is casting the shadows. Plato said most people have no clue there is more to life than the cave's shadowland, but if someone broke free and got outside, they would see the world as it is.

"He will be able to see the sun, and not mere reflections of him in the water, but he will see him in his own proper place, and not in another, and he will contemplate him as he is. He will then argue that this is he who gives the season and the years and is the guardian of all that is in the visible world, and in a certain way the cause of all things he and his fellows have been accustomed to behold."[12]

Known as the "Father of Logic," Aristotle was Plato's student and the tutor of Alexander the Great. In his *Metaphysics*, he argued that an unchanging, eternal, and perfect god is necessary: the

---

[12] Plato, *The Republic*, Book VII, trans. Benjamin Jowett. Internet Classics Archive. http://classics.mit.edu/Plato/republic.9.viii.html

"unmoved mover" who created everything. Aristotle taught the deduction principle: if a premise (belief) is accurate, its conclusion is true. Deduction enables us to understand specific truths and leads us to induction or generalized understanding.

While Athens's philosophers pondered spiritual and scientific truths, the simmering rivalry between Sparta and Athens exploded into the First Peloponnesian War in 460 BCE. At first, Sparta held back while its allies fought Athens, beginning with Corinth. Athens faltered with land wars but won brilliant victories in naval battles. Eventually, Sparta marched to Boeotia, which was sixty miles north of Athens. The Athenians met the Spartans in the Battle of Tanagra, with Sparta emerging as the victor. But Athens's navy was far superior to its land army, so it circled the Peloponnese, raiding Sparta's allies on the coast. At an impasse, Sparta agreed to the Thirty Years' Peace with Athens in 445 BCE, ending the First Peloponnesian War.

The peace only lasted fourteen years, with the Second Peloponnesian War (431–404 BCE) instigated by the Spartans invading the farmland on the Attica Peninsula around Athens. The Spartans stripped their fields, attempting to entice the Athenians into a land battle. But knowing the Spartans' superiority on land, Pericles held back, bringing the rural population into the city walls and holing up, living off of grain shipments from Egypt. Meanwhile, Athens's formidable navy formed a blockade around the Peloponnese, blocking shipments to Sparta and its allies.

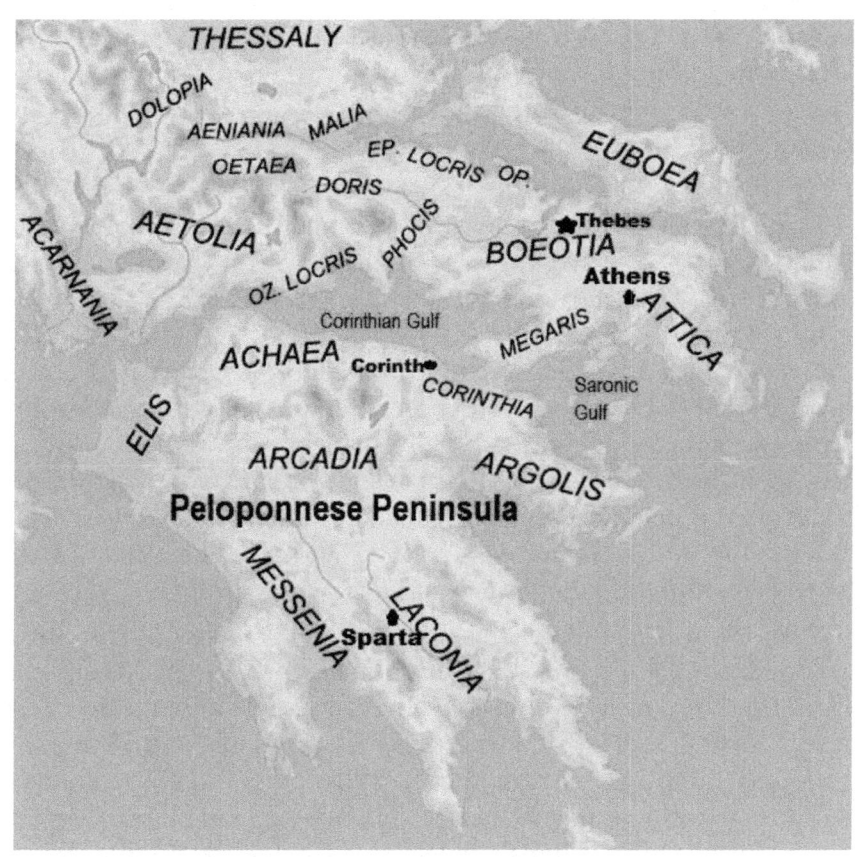

Most of southern Greece was engaged in the Peloponnesian War.
Photo modified: labels added. Credit: original:Map_greek_sanctuaries-en.svg by Marsyasderivative work: MinisterForBadTimes, CC BY-SA 2.5 <https://creativecommons.org/licenses/by-sa/2.5>, via Wikimedia Commons; https://commons.wikimedia.org/wiki/File:Ancient_Greek_southern_regions.png

Pericles never envisioned that the grain shipments from Egypt would bring rats carrying the plague, which spread like wildfire through overcrowded Athens. One-third of the population died from violent diarrhea, tissue death, and lung infection. The survivors burned the dead on pyres or threw them into huge pits by the hundreds each day. As soon as they heard about the outbreak, the Spartans fled the Attica Peninsula. In an ironic twist, the Athenian blockade protected Sparta and the rest of the Peloponnesians from the ships carrying the plague.

Pericles's death from the plague in 429 BCE left Athens without his mature and insightful leadership. But the plague eventually dissipated, and Athens resumed naval raids and fort-building on the Peloponnese. Sparta attacked Pylos, one of these forts, but the Athenians won, the first time they'd prevailed in a land battle with Sparta. This victory empowered and energized the Athenians, as they realized the Spartan army wasn't as invincible as they thought.

Sparta responded to the loss by marching north to Thrace and taking control of Athens's silver mines in Amphipolis. Athens rushed north to regain their primary source of wealth, and in the pitched Battle of Amphipolis, both sides lost their leading generals. In a leadership crisis, the two cities negotiated the fifty-year Peace of Nicias in 421 BCE. But the peace quickly collapsed when some Peloponnese cities abandoned their alliance with Sparta and threw their lot in with Sparta's independent neighbor Argos. The deadly Battle of Mantinea, the largest land battle of the war, ended in a stunning victory for Sparta in 418 BCE, and the defiant cities were forced back into the Peloponnesian League.

Next, the war headed to the island of Sicily, across the Straits of Messina from the toe of Italy's boot. Ionian and Dorian Greeks had colonized Sicily back in the archaic era. Their mother cities were Athens for the Ionians and Sparta for the Dorians, and both cities supported their kinsmen in Sicily. When the Greeks colonized Sicily, they pushed the indigenous people inland. The town of Segesta pleaded for Athens's help against an attack by the Dorian city of Selinus. Athens agreed, and the Sicilian Expedition ensued in 415 BCE, with the Athenians launching an attack on Selinus's ally, Syracuse.

Sparta sent a fleet of eighty ships to Syracuse, and in the first two naval skirmishes, Athens's navy prevailed. But then the Spartan navy trapped the Athenian fleet in the harbor, where they could not maneuver well. Both sides lost about fifty ships in the pitched battle. Finally, the Athenians beached their ships and attempted to escape by land. But the coalition Syracusan-Spartan forces annihilated tens of thousands of the Athenians and enslaved the rest.

Back in Greece, Sparta took control of the northern Attica Peninsula, blocking trade and communications between Athens and northern Greece. Sparta then recaptured Athens's silver mines, leaving Athens financially destitute. Athens demanded more tribute from the Delian League cities, which resulted in the aggrieved

Ionian colonies seceding from the league. The Persians inserted themselves into the war by building warships for Sparta.

In a downward spiral, Athens experienced internal turmoil when a four-hundred-man oligarchy usurped power, its democratic advances melting away. Then, Sparta took control of the Dardanelles, blocking Athens's grain shipments from the Black Sea. When the Athenian navy attempted to break the blockade, the Spartans sank 168 of their 180 ships. In 404 BCE, the Peloponnesian War ended with Athens's surrender. Sparta took the remaining Athenian warships and forced Athens to dismantle its protective walls. Yet, Sparta spared the Athenians from the enslavement proposed by other Greek states, remembering how Athens had rescued Greece from the Persians.

The Delian League, once led by Athens, now fell under Sparta's power. But Sparta didn't just collect tribute; it placed its own governors in the cities, which were supported by Spartan garrisons. Sparta even forced democratic states to become oligarchies. Corinth and Thebes had allied with Sparta in the Peloponnesian War, but they found Sparta's tyranny unacceptable. Persia inserted itself again, hoping to destabilize Greece further by bribing the Greek city-states to revolt against Sparta's power.

King Pausanias of Sparta marched north to meet with Spartan General Lysander, who was returning from Asia, to attack the city of Haliartus, a close ally of Thebes. Lysander arrived first and, without waiting for Pausanias, attacked Haliartus. But suddenly, a Theban army assailed him from the rear. He wasn't aware a Theban army was nearby, which was a fatal mistake since the Thebans cut him down. More Greek city-states switched to the Thebans' side.

The Spartan fleet was returning from the Dardanelles when the Persians and Athenians suddenly attacked it. General Conon of Athens commanded one Persian fleet, while Persian Governor Pharnabazus of Phrygia (in western Turkey) commanded a Phoenician fleet. The Spartans ran their ships up on the shore and fled, with the Persians and Athenians close behind. The beach ran red with Greek blood, and Sparta's naval empire folded.

General Conon and his new Persian friend Pharnabazus wreaked havoc on the Peloponnese coast and then sailed to Athens, where Pharnabazus financed the rebuilding of Athens's walls. But

Sparta was still blocking Athens's grain shipments, so in 387 BCE, the Persians finally negotiated the King's Peace with Sparta, Athens, Argos, Corinth, and Thebes. The Persians got Cyprus and the Ionian Greek colonies in Asia, but all other Greek city-states were now independently ruled.

Sparta broke the treaty five years later by attacking Thebes and establishing a garrison there. But the Theban leaders had secretly trained young men in combat skills, and in 379 BCE, they killed the Spartan leaders but permitted the rest of the soldiers at the garrison to leave unharmed. Winning a land battle against the Spartans galvanized the Thebans into forming a three-hundred-man Sacred Band with highly-skilled full-time warriors. Meanwhile, Athens staged a comeback in the next decade, creating the Second Athenian League in 378 BCE. Unlike the first, all the city-states maintained their independence in a decentralized alliance.

Sparta's power over the other Greek city-states finally imploded at the 371 BCE Battle of Leuctra. The Spartans marched north to attack Thebes and caught the Thebans unaware, but the Thebans quickly rallied seven miles south of Thebes. The Thebans used their new intimidating fifty-man-deep phalanx formation and spine-chilling twelve-foot-long spears. Thebes' crushing triumph allowed it to dominate Greece for the next decade as they won one battle after another.

Thebes invaded Thessaly and Macedon to the north, taking Macedon's adolescent prince, Philip II, as a hostage, with no inkling of how that would one day change the course of history. As Thebes became stronger, a nervous Athens allied with Sparta in the consequential 362 BCE Battle of Mantinea. Thebes won the brutal battle but at a grievous cost, losing their seasoned war leader Epaminondas.

Thebes successfully invaded Sparta and freed their helots, who did Sparta's manual work. Without their helot labor freeing the Spartan men to be full-time warriors, Sparta's army floundered. But Thebes also struggled, having lost its expert generals. Neither Sparta nor Thebes could maintain control over the rest of Greece, leaving the door open for Macedon's rising star: Philip II.

Chapter 5: Philip II and Alexander the Great

"Sire, you have another letter from King Darius. He's offering peace terms again."

"I'm sure he is!" Alexander the Great chuckled. "I've conquered the entire Mediterranean coast, and I've got his women! Can you believe he abandoned them on the battlefield?"

"Yes, he asks that you return his mother, wife, and daughters. In return, you will receive half the Persian Empire, a gold fortune, and one of his daughters in marriage."

"Ha!" Alexander laughed. "I already have all that! I've got the gold of Lydia, Tyre, and Egypt. I have both his daughters, and I've conquered half the empire. Why should I stop now when I can have it all?"

Who would believe that obscure Macedon on Greece's northern frontier would rise to such heights? While Sparta, Thebes, and Athens fought for control, Macedon was nothing but a backwater at risk of being absorbed by stronger powers. And yet, under Philip II, it rose to conquer most of the Greek mainland; under Philip's son Alexander, it conquered the entire Persian Empire.

Political chaos marked Philip II's childhood and youth. After the assassination of his oldest brother, King Alexander II, he spent his teen years as a hostage in Thebes. But Theban General

Epaminondas schooled him in diplomacy and Theban military arts. Philip dreamed of reforming Macedon's military as he studied the Theban phalanx formation and weaponry. At the age of twenty-three, Philip unexpectantly became Macedon's king when his brother, King Perdiccas III, died in battle.

Philip immediately set to work transforming Macedon's military. He trained his soldiers with the sarissa: a deadly twenty-foot-long spear he invented. The men also learned Philip's innovative phalanx: sixteen rows of men eight men wide, giving them superior maneuverability. Philip quickly began expanding Macedon's borders, avenging his brother's death, and defeating the surrounding nations that had once threatened his kingdom's existence. He spread his kingdom west, encompassing today's Albania, east into today's Bulgaria, and north into today's Serbia and Kosovo. He took control of Athens's silver mines in Amphipolis.

By the end of his reign, Philip II controlled most of the Balkan Peninsula.
Photo modified: zoomed in and labels added. Credit: ArnoldPlaton, CC BY-SA 3.0
<https://creativecommons.org/licenses/by-sa/3.0>, via Wikimedia Commons
https://commons.wikimedia.org/wiki/File:Balkan_Peninsula.svg

Although the Greeks only had one wife at a time, the Macedonian noblemen married multiple wives to form strategic alliances. In 337 BCE, Philip married his fourth wife, Princess Olympias of Epirus, and she gave birth to their son Alexander the following year. Philip hired the renowned philosopher Aristotle to tutor Alexander and invited the Greek rulers to send their sons to study with Alexander under Aristotle, leading to astute Greek alliances.

Philip's next military target was the Greek city-states to the south. His opportunity came when the Third Sacred War broke out in 356 BCE at Delphi in central Greece. Pythia, the Oracle of Delphi, was a priestess who would go into a trance after breathing in fumes from a fissure underneath the Temple of Apollo. People from around the Greek world traveled to Delphi to seek her advice. The city of Phocis had dared to plow farms in the sacred precinct around Delphi and then committed greater sacrilege by raiding the Temple of Apollo and stealing its treasures.

Defending Delphi not only gave Philip hero status to Apollo's worshipers but also allowed him to gain control in central Greece. Philip had been fighting Thessaly at his southern border but suddenly offered to ally with it to fight for Delphi. Together, they crushed Phocis, wiping out its military. The Thessalonians were so impressed with Philip's leadership that they made him their chief magistrate for life.

Part of Philip's peace settlement with Phocis was control of the Thermopylae Pass, which lay in Phocis' land, giving him unhindered access to southern Greece. To prevent him from invading, Athens negotiated a settlement with Philip, which he was happy to do. Philip needed Athens's navy for his long-term goal of invading and conquering the Persian Empire with a united Greek force.

Isocrates, the influential orator of Athens, encouraged Philip in his quest. "You must reconcile the four great Greek cities: Argos, Athens, Sparta, and Thebes. If they unite, everyone else will join in. We must stop this constant infighting between the Greek city-states and bring them together to fight Persia!"

Philip II's image on a gold stater coin.

But the Athenian statesman Demosthenes ranted, "Philip is the worst enemy Athens could have! He's a despot! We need to fight the Macedonians, not collude with them."

While Philip fought the Persians at Byzantium (later known as Constantinople), where Europe and Asia join, Demosthenes convinced Athens to ally with Persia against Philip. Philip desperately needed control of Byzantium because it would be his route to the Persian Empire. Exasperated with Athens, Philip marched back to Greece as Athens quickly allied with Thebes to fend him off. Thebes blocked Philip from the Thermopylae Pass, but Philip knew about the alternative route.

Philip crossed the mountains and faced off with Athens, Corinth, and Thebes in the Battle of Chaeronea. His eighteen-year-old son, Alexander, commanded the left flank with assistance from experienced officers, and Philip commanded the right side. The Greek forces lined up on the road in a two-and-a-half-mile formation, with the Thebans on the right flank against Alexander, the Athenians on an incline across from Philip, and the Corinthians in the middle.

Philip didn't want the Athenians to have the uphill advantage, so he quickly engaged and then feigned a retreat. The Athenians chased Philip's forces across the narrow valley and up the hill on the other side. Philip whirled his troops around to fight, with the

Athenians now downhill, making them an easier target for his archers. On the left flank, young Alexander proved his skills by shattering the Thebans' legendary Sacred Band.

Athens and Corinth were dumbfounded when Philip did not flatten their cities. But that wasn't his plan. He wanted the Greek states to unite under his leadership to fight Persia. He desired to fight *with* them, not destroy them. Philip was more concerned about Sparta, which had remained uninvolved. What if Sparta started wreaking havoc on Greece's cities while their forces were overseas fighting Persia? In laconic Spartan fashion, they refused negotiations.

However, the rest of Greece was ready to come to the table. They formed the League of Corinth in 337 BCE, where all the city-states (except Sparta) agreed not to fight each other but to unite against Persia. They formally declared war on the Persian Empire, making Philip their commander. Within months, Philip sent General Parmenion to Asia to free the Greek city-states in Ionia from Persian rule. But then disaster struck.

Philip was throwing a wedding for his daughter Cleopatra to her uncle, King Alexander of Epirus. As Philip entered the hall, his bodyguard and jilted lover, Pausanias, suddenly thrust a dagger into his ribs. The great warrior was dead! What would happen now? Would the Macedonian-Greek alliance still invade the Achaemenid Empire? Who would lead them?

While Philip lay bleeding out, the Macedonian military and nobles wasted no time declaring Alexander as their next king. The twenty-year-old had multiple calamities demanding his immediate attention. As soon as they heard of Philip's death, several Greek cities dropped out of the League of Corinth. Alexander had to rein them in quickly to proceed with the Persian invasion.

Alexander marched south, where the Thessalian forces waited at the Mount Olympus Pass. But he took a circuitous route and unexpectantly came up on their rear the following morning. Taken off guard, Thebes surrendered, and Alexander continued south, where Athens and Corinth apologetically acknowledged his rule. Alexander then headed north to bring Thrace and northern Greece into line.

Alexander spent the next year pummeling the northern rebels into submission, but Thebes and Athens backed out of the League of Corinth again. This time, Alexander was not so ready to forgive. He demolished the city of Thebes, sparing only the temples. He enslaved its citizens and donated its land to the surrounding towns. Athens promptly sent envoys to Alexander, pleading for mercy, which Alexander granted.

With all of Greece (except Sparta) united again, Alexander embarked on his audacious invasion of the Persian Empire. In 334 BCE, he led forty thousand Greeks and Macedonians across the Hellespont into Asia, pausing in Troy to honor the heroes of the ancient war. King Darius III of Persia wasn't especially worried. He didn't even leave Persia, assuming his governors' forces could easily repel the Greeks and Macedonians in Ionia.

General Memnon of Rhodes did not share King Darius's optimism. He had escaped to Macedon as a young man following a failed revolt against Persia's former king. He was a personal acquaintance of Philip II and his son Alexander and knew their grandiose plans. He also knew what their military machine could do. He advised the Persian satraps (governors), "We need a scorched-earth policy! Get the people off the coast! Leave nothing behind that the Greeks and their horses can eat. He needs to feed his people and their animals. Starve him, and he'll leave!"

The Persians ignored his advice. Why should they run away? They could send this upstart Macedonian packing! Instead, they lined up at the Granicus River to square off with Alexander. The Greeks would have to cross the sixty-foot-wide, swiftly flowing river, then climb up a steep bluff to meet the Persian military. As Alexander's forces drew near, the sun was about to set. Surely, he would wait until morning to cross.

But no! Instead, the Macedonian-Greek forces quickly moved into position. Alexander led the right flank with his Macedonian cavalry, elite infantry, archers, and javelin throwers. His formidable infantry formed the Macedonian phalanx in the center, and his Thessalian-Thracian cavalry took the left flank. As Alexander's right-flank cavalry plunged into the river, the Persians responded with a hail of arrows that darkened the sun.

Alexander and his horsemen galloped across the river and up the steep bank, fending off the Persians' attempts to push them down into the river. Alexander speared King Darius's son-in-law Mithridates, but then the satrap Spithridates smashed Alexander's helmet with his battle ax. The helmet fell away in two pieces but did not greatly injure Alexander. Alexander's close friend Black Cleitus impaled Spithridates before he could strike again. Meanwhile, the rest of Alexander's army was wading through the river's swift current and clambering up the embankment to form ranks with their twenty-foot sarissas. The Persians took one look at the wall of spears and panicked, running off the battlefield.

After this victory, the Ionian city-states surrendered to Alexander. Alexander next assailed Miletus and Halicarnassus, Persia's major ports, crippling Persia's naval fleet. As Alexander passed through the city of Gordium, someone pointed out the Gordian Knot, telling their leader about the prophecy. Whoever untied the massive tangle would rule Asia. Alexander smiled and slashed the knot in two with his sword. Asia was his! Most scholars conclude that this story is a myth.

This Pompey mural depicts Alexander at the Battle of Issus.

By this point, King Darius realized he needed to lead his military in person. As Alexander marched south along the Mediterranean, King Darius unexpectantly came up on his rear, trapping Alexander's men on a narrow plain between the Nur Mountains and the Gulf of Issus. Alexander wheeled around, and his well-trained military immediately fell into the same formation they used at the Granicus River.

On the Pinarus River's northern banks, Darius's heavy cavalry lined up next to the sea. The Persians had been hiring Greek soldiers as mercenaries for over a century, and in this battle, Darius's Greek infantry in the center faced off against their fellow Greeks. The Persian infantry extended up into the foothills, and a contingent crossed the river in an attempt to outflank the Macedonians' right wing. The Persian cavalry plunged across the river, confronting General Parmenion's Thessalian-Thracian cavalry.

The Macedonian cavalry raced over the river, breaking through the Persian infantry's left wing. But Alexander's center infantry, weighed down with their shields and heavy sarissas, were daunted by the swift current and retreated from the river. But Alexander led his elite right-flank infantry across the river unchallenged because the Macedonian cavalry had disrupted the Persian infantry facing him.

Once over the river, Alexander leaped onto a horse and charged straight at King Darius, with his Macedonian horsemen right behind him. Darius panicked and fled the field in his chariot. Once word swept through the Persian ranks that their king had abandoned them, they raced off, with the Greeks close behind, killing anyone who couldn't run fast enough.

Although injured, Alexander scored a tremendous victory in the Battle of Issus. He even captured Darius's womenfolk in the Persian camp; Persian women often accompanied their male relatives to battle. When Darius and his men ran for the hills, they left behind Darius's queen, the queen mother, and his two daughters. Alexander took them into his custody, treating them with respect. Several months later, Darius's wife died in childbirth, and Alexander gave her a royal funeral. He later married one of the daughters, Stateira II.

As Alexander's horde of warriors headed south along Lebanon's coast in 332 BCE, all the Phoenician cities except ancient Tyre surrendered. Tyre had built a new city on an island a half-mile offshore with 150-foot walls. As Alexander approached, the city evacuated their women and children to Carthage in Africa.

Alexander laid siege to the city for seven months, building a causeway to the island with rubble from the old Tyre. But the sea suddenly dropped to eighteen feet deep as they got farther offshore. So, Alexander rounded up 220 ships from Cyprus, Ionia, and other Phoenician cities. Six thousand Tyrians died as the Macedonians and Greeks took the city. Alexander crucified another two thousand and enslaved thirty thousand.

Egypt had chafed under Persian rule and attempted multiple times to regain independence. Now, they welcomed Alexander as their deliverer from the Achaemenid Empire. They handed over their treasury, and the priests crowned him as Egypt's new pharaoh. At the mouth of the Nile, Alexander built the new city of Alexandria, which grew into a breathtaking center of Hellenistic culture and scientific study.

Darius met Alexander with elephants and scythed chariots.

King Darius clashed with Alexander a final time in 331 BCE at the Battle of Gaugamela in today's northern Iraq. The Macedonians and Greeks faced war elephants from India this time, which was a new experience for them. Darius had another new weapon: four-horsed scythed chariots. Their blades extended three feet out from the wheels' hubs and could slice a man's leg in half. Alexander led a cavalry charge around the Persian left flank, drawing them toward him and thinning out the defense in the center where King Darius was.

The Persian scythed chariots pressed toward the Greeks, but with the flexible Macedonian phalanx, the Greeks stepped aside to allow the chariots to pass through as the Bulgarian javelin throwers impaled the horses and their drivers. As the center line surrounding Darius disintegrated, Darius abandoned the field, with his men fleeing when they realized their king had left them.

Alexander headed south to Babylon, where he was hailed as the Persian Empire's new king. Darius fled east, hoping to recruit more men and retake his kingdom, but his Bactrian satrap Bessus murdered him. After arranging a proper royal funeral, Alexander appointed leadership over his new lands, keeping the governors in place who acknowledged him as their king. Next, Alexander marched east. His first objective was to find and execute Bessus. He then wanted to explore and conquer east to "the edge of the world," the Ganges River in the Indian subcontinent.

The Bactrian chieftains turned Bessus over to Alexander, who then gave him to King Darius's brother to supervise his crucifixion. While in Bactria (today's Afghanistan and Tajikistan), Alexander met Roxana, the daughter of the Bactrian chieftain Oxyartes. For Alexander, it was love at first sight. He married the young girl, despite his friends' objections, who felt he should marry a Macedonian princess or at least Darius's daughter. In their minds, Roxana's family wasn't prestigious enough for the new emperor. Alexander then marched to the Achaemenid Empire's easternmost border at the Jaxartes River.

By this time, his troops were weary and demoralized, having been away from their families for ten years. They were also wary of Alexander's abrupt mood changes, especially after he got drunk and killed his good friend Cleitus the Black. But Alexander ignored their protests and pressed on, scaling the 3,500-foot Khyber Pass over the Hindu Kush range and descending into today's Pakistan.

Alexander's hopes of traveling to the great river of India were dashed when his men rebelled. They were obstinate; it was time to go home! Alexander was livid but gave in and accompanied his men back to Babylon. When they arrived, Alexander threw a collective wedding, marrying eighty Persian princesses to his officers, uniting the Macedonian, Greek, and Persian royal families. Alexander married two princesses that day: Darius's daughter, Stateira, and Parysatis, the daughter of an earlier Persian king, Artaxerxes III.

In 323 BCE, Alexander was elated with the news that his first wife, Roxanna, was pregnant. But several months later, he became ill with a fever and died within two weeks. He had never lost a major battle. He reaped one staggering victory over another as he built a sensational three-continent empire. But he died before he could effectively rule it or name a successor. What would happen to Greece, Macedonia, Egypt, and his new Asian provinces now?

Chapter 6: The Diadochi and the Roman Conquest

Alexander's top generals met to discuss the unexpected leadership crisis of Alexander's new empire. General Perdiccas held up Alexander's ring, "Our commander and king, Alexander, gave this to me before he died. I'm to be the regent for his half-brother Arrhidaeus and for Roxana's child."

"Arrhidaeus? He's mentally deficient! How can he rule?"

"He's Alexander's closest male relative," Perdiccas explained. "Yes, he has physical and mental challenges, but we can guide him. He will marry his niece, Princess Eurydice. Roxana is due to give birth soon. If it's a girl, we'll make Arrhidaeus king, and if it's a boy, Alexander's son will be king."

"Ha! As regent, you'll be the de facto king either way," one of the generals pointed out. "So, how does Arrhidaeus feel about all this? Does he even want to be king?"

General Meleager went out to fetch Arrhidaeus. When Meleager returned with the young man, Arrhidaeus was overwhelmed at the sight of his brother's stern generals and ducked out, quivering in fear. They coaxed him back in, but tears flowed down Arrhidaeus's face. "I'm unqualified to be your king."

One of the generals asked, "Why can't we have two kings?"

The generals finally agreed on the Partition of Babylon, in which Arrhidaeus would co-reign with Roxana's baby if it were a boy. Perdiccas would be the regent for the kings and command the empire's army. As Alexander's Diadochi or successors, the other generals divided sections of the empire among themselves to rule. Two months later, Roxana gave birth to a boy, King Alexander IV.

The other generals rebelled against Perdiccas in the First War of the Diadochi (322–319 BCE) because he wanted to marry Alexander the Great's sister Cleopatra and become Macedon's king. Then Perdiccas marched against General Ptolemy, now Egypt's pharaoh, who stole Alexander's body to honor Alexander's request for burial in Egypt. But Perdiccas's men rebelled, and his three leading officers killed him, ending the first war.

With Perdiccas dead, the generals made new arrangements for the regency of the two kings. In the 321 BCE Partition of Triparadisus, Queen Eurydice became the de facto regent for her husband, Arrhidaeus. Antipater, who Alexander had appointed as regent of Macedonia while he invaded Persia, became regent over Roxana's toddler son, King Alexander IV. Antipater brought the two kings and the queen to Macedon. General Seleucus, one of Perdiccas's murderers, became Babylon's ruler. He would eventually rule as king of the Seleucid Empire, which encompassed most of the Middle East.

Two years later, Antipater died, leaving General Polyperchon as the new regent. But Antipater's son Cassander felt the regency was rightfully his and allied with Ptolemy and General Antigonus the One-Eye to evict Polyperchon from Macedon. Polyperchon escaped to Epirus with Roxana and her four-year-old boy, Alexander IV, and the three generals made Arrhidaeus the sole king of the empire.

But Alexander the Great's mother, Olympias, allied with Polyperchon in a battle against King Arrhidaeus and Queen Eurydice. The Macedonian soldiers refused to fight Queen Mother Olympias, who ordered the deaths of Arrhidaeus and Eurydice. Yet Olympias's victory was short-lived. Cassander allied with Antigonus, Ptolemy, and another of Alexander's generals, Lysimachus. They defeated Olympias, and she was stoned to death in 316 BCE. Cassander captured Roxana and the boy-king Alexander, locking them in a tower in Macedonia for years. The Second Diadochi War ended with victory for the four generals.

King Alexander IV was about to turn fourteen. He would soon be old enough to rule without a regent. Cassander poisoned him and Roxana in 309 BCE but kept their murders a secret, although it hardly mattered by this time. The five Diadochi who remained were now calling themselves king, indicating independence from the empire. Antigonus ruled from western Turkey to Egypt's border, and Cassander ruled Macedon and Thessaly. Lysimachus had Thrace, Seleucus controlled the Middle East (from Iraq to Afghanistan), and Ptolemy was pharaoh over Egypt and Libya.

The final clash in the 301 BCE Battle of Ipsus in Phrygia (western Turkey) ended the Wars of the Diadochi. Cassander, Lysimachus, and Seleucus allied against Antigonus. Seleucus was on his way back from a campaign in India and brought five hundred war elephants. As Lysimachus attacked western Turkey, Antigonus's son Demetrius rushed over from Greece to assist his father in Ipsus.

Antigonus and Demetrius had seventy-five war elephants, which they sent out in the opening charge. They were met by two hundred of Seleucus's elephants. Antigonus's stronger infantry prevailed until Seleucus released his other three hundred elephants. Seleucus's cavalry outflanked Antigonus's right wing. A javelin struck and killed Antigonus. Demetrius escaped to Greece, where he would plot a successful takeover of Macedonia.

Cassander and Ptolemy died of natural causes in 297 and 282, respectively. Only Seleucus and Lysimachus remained of the original reigning generals. Seleucus marched against Lysimachus in 281 BCE, and Lysimachus died in the battle. But a few months later, Ptolemy I's son, Ptolemy Ceraunus, assassinated Seleucus, the last of the Diadochi.

Seleucus was the last of Alexander the Great's generals.

The dynamic Hellenistic (Greek) culture permeated Asia, Africa, and eastern Europe. The Greeks assimilated the cultures of the people they led, blending Middle Eastern, Egyptian, and Indian influences with Greek art, philosophy, science, and mathematics. The Greek cities of Alexandria, Egypt, and Antioch, Syria, were the new scientific and artistic powerhouses.

Alexandria on the Nile Delta had a half million people and a thriving sea trade around the Mediterranean. Its priceless library held thousands of scrolls on history, science, religion, and literature. Its chief librarian, Eratosthenes, calculated the earth's circumference at being 28,000 to 29,000 miles, astoundingly close to today's calculations of 24,901 miles. Aristarchus of Samos taught that the earth circled the sun once a year and rotated on its axis on a twenty-four-hour day.

Archimedes of Syracuse devised a formula for determining the volume of a sphere and calculated pi (π) to 3.14 for the ratio of a circle's diameter to its circumference. He is called the founder of theoretical mechanics for developing the law of the lever. He also developed Archimedes' principle: a solid placed in a fluid is lighter by the fluid weight it displaces. He demonstrated how he could move a ship with a compound pulley.

Alexander the Great and his Hellenistic successors spread the Koine Greek dialect as the common language throughout the Mediterranean and the Middle East. A shared language enhanced trade and enabled discussions between scientific, mathematic, and religious scholars. Ptolemy II, Egypt's second Macedonian pharaoh, commissioned Jewish scholars to translate the Tanakh (Old Testament) into Koine Greek. Known as the Septuagint translation, it became the standard version used in synagogues throughout North Africa and the Middle East.

Hellenism introduced a new era of Greek sculptures. While archaic era sculptures featured stiff young women and men with slight smiles, classical Greek sculptures featured perfect bodies in sinuous and fluid motion. The Hellenistic sculptures portrayed people with imperfections, extreme emotions, flexed musculature, and exaggerated action. A dramatic example is the Laocoön Group, which features the violent deaths of the Trojan priest Laocoön and his two sons by serpents.

The Laocoön sculpture demonstrates the agony of death and despair
https://commons.wikimedia.org/wiki/File:Laocoon_Vatican_detail.jpg

The Greek world first clashed with Rome in 280 BCE. The Roman Republic had been confined to central Italy, but now it was conquering territory and extending into southern Italy. Greece had colonized southernmost Italy (the toe and heel of Italy's boot) in the archaic era. Now, several wealthy and powerful Greek city-states controlled the sea trade in the region.

"One more victory like that, and we're finished!" When King Pyrrhus of Epirus inserted himself into Italy's political scene, he discovered that a technical win could be so costly that it was a "Pyrrhic victory." It all started when Rome broke a treaty with southern Italy's powerful Greek city-state of Tarentum by sailing ten ships into the Gulf of Taranto. Tarentum angrily responded by sinking four Roman vessels, and Rome declared war.

When the Tarentines asked King Pyrrhus of Epirus in northwestern Greece for assistance, he jumped at his chance to get a foothold in Italy. A relative of Alexander the Great, he harbored ambitions of building his own empire, despite lacking soldiers, funding, and ships. He borrowed all that from Macedonia, the Seleucid Empire, and Egypt, sailing to Italy in 280 BCE. To the Tarentines' dismay, he cracked down on frivolities and drafted the men into his army.

Pyrrhus first confronted Rome in the Battle of Heraclea at the Siris River. His initial cavalry charge broke through the Roman lines. Horrified by the Roman ferocity, he demanded his lieutenant exchange armor with him. Thinking the lieutenant was King Pyrrhus, the Romans quickly killed him. Pyrrhus's war elephants turned the tide of the battle, terrifying the Roman soldiers and their horses. The Greeks won, but both sides suffered catastrophic losses: fifteen thousand Roman deaths to thirteen thousand Greeks.

Over the winter, Pyrrhus recruited troops from Ionia and Macedonia, building his military to forty thousand soldiers. He warred with Rome again in 279 BCE in a grueling two-day battle that raged in wooded terrain this time, impeding horse and elephant charges. The Romans further obstructed elephant charges by lining up three hundred anti-elephant oxcarts with spears poking out and catapults to hurl stones at the Greeks.

King Pyrrhus fought for Italy's Greek city-states against Rome.

Pyrrhus guided his elephants around the end of the anti-elephant wagons on the second day. One look at the elephants and the spooked Roman horses raced off. Technically, Pyrrhus won again: the Romans lost seven thousand men, and the Greeks lost about half that. But Pyrrhus was wounded, and most of his commanders were dead.

Pyrrhus's physician, Nicias, approached the Romans, offering to kill King Pyrrhus. The Roman commanders warned Pyrrhus in a letter:

"We, being greatly disturbed in spirit because of your continued acts of injustice, desire to war with you as an enemy. But as a matter of general precedent and honor, it has seemed to us that we should desire your personal safety in order that we may have the opportunity of vanquishing you in the field."[13]

Pyrrhus thanked the Romans by freeing his Roman prisoners of war. He executed Nicias, forming the straps of a chair from his flayed skin. Then, he surprised everyone by suddenly leaving Italy and sailing to Sicily to assist the Greek city-states in their struggle against Carthage. The Sicilian Greeks said he could be their king if he rid Sicily of the Carthaginians. In his absence, Rome brought the southern Italian tribes in line and overpowered all of Italy's Greek city-states except for Rhegion and Tarentum.

Pyrrhus's Sicilian venture ended in dismal failure, and the remnants of his fleet sailed back to Italy in 276 BCE. He marched by night toward the Roman forces at Maleventum, planning a surprise attack at dawn. But his men wandered off the path into goat trails in the dark. When the weary soldiers finally came out of the woods at Maleventum, they were on a high hill in full view of the Roman troops. The Greeks suffered a brutal loss, and Pyrrhus left Italy for good. Rome now ruled all the Greek cities in southern Italy.

Rome's first offshore war was with Carthage in a successful bid to gain control of Sicily's Greek city-states. In the First Punic War (264–241 BCE), Rome forced Carthage to abandon Sicily. While

---

[13]A. Cornelius Gellius, *Noctes Atticae* (Attic Nights), Volume I, Book III (Loeb Classical Library). http://penelope.uchicago.edu/Thayer/E/Roman/Texts/Gellius/3*.html#8

battling Carthage, Rome also warred on Greece's mainland for the first time when Rome inserted itself into the convoluted politics of the Macedonian Wars.

Hannibal of Carthage had surprised Rome by crossing the Alps and swooping down on Italy from its northern border. While Hannibal was wreaking havoc in Italy, King Philip V of Macedonia allied with him to rid the eastern Adriatic Sea of Roman influence. Hannibal was too busy in Italy and Carthage to help, but Rome intercepted their communications and found out about the alliance. Rome then allied with central Greece's Aetolian League against Philip V.

The Aetolian League attacked central Greece's Acarnania, which had allied with Philip. The Acarnanians were winning until the Roman navy sailed in, captured several of their cities, and enslaved the people. Sparta jumped into the fray, allying with the Aetolian League and Rome, but Philip defeated the allied Greeks in the Peloponnese in 209 BCE. This spurred King Attalus I of Pergamon to unite with the Aetolian League, and his navy joined Rome in patrolling the Aegean Sea.

But when Bithynia invaded Pergamum, Attalus had to rush home. Rome's simultaneous war with Carthage forced it to divert its navy from the Aegean Sea, which gave Philip free rein to capture cities in the Gulf of Corinth. When Philip's allies killed Sparta's tyrant, Machanidas, Sparta pulled out of the war, empowering Philip to expel the Aetolian League from Ionia and Thessaly. The Aetolian League conceded to Philip, ending the First Macedonian War in 205 BCE.

The Second Macedonian War began in 200 BCE with a clandestine conspiracy between Philip V and the Seleucid Empire's King Antiochus to steal Egypt's throne. The Macedonian Ptolemy V had inherited Egypt's throne at the age of five, and a series of bungling regents had destabilized Egypt. The two kings agreed that if their plot succeeded, Antiochus would annex Egypt into the Seleucid Empire; Philip would get Cyrene and Egypt's holdings in the Aegean Sea.

Antiochus immediately set to work, conquering his way down the Mediterranean coast, taking the Egyptian-held cities of Damascus, Sidon, and Samaria. The Jews threw open Jerusalem's gates to

Antiochus, celebrating their emancipation from Egypt, little suspecting the horrors his son would one day inflict. Meanwhile, Philip conquered Egypt's Aegean naval base of Samos and its neighboring territory in Miletus.

Rome finally crushed Carthage, ending the Third Punic War. Now it had the ships and manpower to focus on Greece and Macedonia. Rome ordered Philip to abandon all aggressions against Greek and Egyptian territories. If he complied, he could retain Macedonia and Thrace. The Roman ambassador Lepidus personally delivered the ultimatum to Philip in the final days of his siege of the city of Abydos, which would give him control of the Dardanelles.

King Philip answered Lepidus, "I pardon the offensive haughtiness of your manners for three reasons: first, because you are a young man and inexperienced in affairs; secondly, because you are the most handsome man of your time [this was true]; and thirdly, because you are a Roman."[14]

Abydos fell to Philip. Rather than face enslavement, the men killed their wives and children, throwing them from rooftops or into wells, and then stabbed or burned themselves to death. Rome responded by sending Consul Sulpicius to attack Philip in Epirus. After a few inconclusive clashes, Philip received news that the Dardanians of the central Balkans were invading Macedon, so he immediately left to defend his country.

Philip met his match in 198 BCE when Rome's new consul, Titus Quinctius Flamininus, dislodged him from Greece. As he was marching through Albania back to Macedonia, Flamininus caught Philip off guard with a rear attack, slaughtering two thousand of his men. The following year, Philip faced off again with Flamininus in the Battle of Cynoscephalae in a fog-covered valley in Thessaly. Philip's men heard the eerie sound of elephants trumpeting; this was the first time Rome used war elephants. The terrified Macedonians could hear the elephants' lumbering feet but couldn't

---

[14] Polybius, *Histories,* Book 16.
http://www.perseus.tufts.edu/hopper/text?doc=Perseus%3Atext%3A1999.01.0234%3Aboo
k%3D16%3Achapter%3D34

see anything until the elephants charged at them through the dense mist. The Romans killed eight thousand Macedonians that day, and the Second Macedonian War ended with Philip's surrender and the loss of his navy and army.

Philip V faced Rome's war elephants at the Battle of Cynoscephalae.
Bernard Picart, Public domain;
https://commons.wikimedia.org/wiki/File:Eleazars_exploit.jpg

After Philip's death, his aggressive son Perseus rallied Thrace's Odrysian Kingdom and some of the Greek city-states by promising to return Greece to its former dominance and splendor. He instigated the Third Macedonian War (171–168 BCE) by conquering northern Thessaly. Rome responded by sending troops to Thessaly, but in the Battle of Callinicus, the Macedonians killed two thousand Romans while suffering only four hundred Macedonian casualties.

When the Romans scavenged the crops in the region, Perseus attacked the Roman camp, capturing the six hundred Romans left behind and Roman supplies. He didn't realize Rome's consul, Publius Licinius Crassus, was in the area until Crassus charged in with his war elephants and Numidian cavalry, killing eight thousand Macedonians.

In another nightmarish loss on Macedonia's coast in 168 BCE, Perseus fled the Battle of Pydna, leaving his men behind for the Romans to massacre or enslave. The Romans finally found him on the island of Samothrace and hauled him to Rome. They paraded him through the streets before throwing him into prison, where he spent the rest of his life. Rome divided Macedon into four republics.

In 146 BCE, the Achaean League in Greece's Peloponnese rebelled against their former ally Rome because Rome forbade any expansion of their territory. Rome crushed the Greeks' main force at the Battle of Scarpheia. Most Greeks killed themselves or fled to Corinth, where the final battle destroyed the city, and the Romans stripped its priceless sculptures and treasures. The rest of the city-states acknowledged Rome's dominion. Yet, Greece continued to impact Rome's philosophy, art, literature, and politics for centuries, spreading its culture as the Roman Republic (and later empire) grew.

PART THREE:
The Roman and Byzantine Periods (146 BCE–1453 CE)

Chapter 7: The Greco-Roman World and Early Byzantine Years

What happened to Greece and the Hellenistic empires after they fell to Rome? Did they retain their culture? Why did the "Greek" side of the Roman Empire persist into the Middle Ages when the Western Roman Empire collapsed? In what ways did the new Christian religion impact the Greek world, and how did the Koine Greek language enable it to spread?

Rome ruled the Greek world for five centuries; however, Greek civilization continued to greatly impact Roman culture, just as it had since Rome's earliest history. The Greeks had colonized southern Italy in the 8th century BCE, about the same time as Rome's founding in central Italy. The Romans traded with southern Italy's Greek city-states and later with the rest of the Greek world, assimilating Greek culture.

Through the centuries, the Romans integrated Greek mythology, political ideas, philosophy, art, and architecture into their culture. The austere Romans especially admired the Greek Stoic philosophers who disdained frivolous luxuries while promoting logic and self-sacrifice. The Romans brought Greek prisoners of war back to Rome, many of whom were highly educated. These enslaved Greek intellectuals tutored the children of the Roman elite in the Greek language and literature. A status symbol for elite Romans was the ability to read and write in Greek and having knowledge of the Greek classics.

When Rome conquered Corinth and other Greek cities, it hauled priceless art and statuary back to Rome, seriously damaging the exquisite pieces in transport. However, the Romans used the Greek spoils of war as models, studying and copying the works. Free Greeks began moving to Rome to work as artists or physicians, which were in high demand. The Greco-Roman blend of Greek and Roman culture spread through the territories that Rome conquered, from Britain to central Asia.

After "freeing" Greece from Macedonian dominance, Rome initially avoided direct rule over Greece, allowing political autonomy. But in 146 BCE, Rome obliterated Corinth as a lesson against rebellion and established the Roman province of Macedonia, which initially included the previous country of Macedonia and most of today's Greece. Caesar Augustus (r. 27 BCE–14 CE) separated mainland Greece and the Cyclades from Macedonia, forming the new Roman province of Achaea.

The Hellenistic Kingdom of Pontus (today's western Turkey) revolted against Rome in the First Mithridatic War (89–85 BCE). In May 88 BCE, King Mithridates ordered an ethnic cleansing of all Romans in Pontus, killing at least eighty thousand men, women, and children on the same day. He took control of much of Greece, installing Aristion as Athens's tyrant. Rome's consul Sulla marched on Greece in 87 BCE, with most Greek cities quickly capitulating. But Athens resisted, resulting in a five-month siege of the city that ended with its fall on March 1ˢᵗ, 86 BCE. The streets of Athens flowed with blood as the Romans sacked and burned. After this horror, Greece carefully maintained compliance with Rome.

Once Greece submitted to Rome, it enjoyed an unprecedented two centuries of relative peace in the Pax Romana (Roman Peace, 27 BCE–180 CE). Rome's rule over a vast territory, stretching from the Middle East to western Europe, facilitated stability, prosperous trade, and population growth. It was an era when the arts, literature, science, and technology reached new heights, as people from three continents freely interacted and exchanged ideas.

The Romans freely copied Greek drama, sculpture, literature, philosophy, and rhetoric, putting their spin on Hellenistic culture, yet the Greeks were largely disinterested in reciprocating. Although they learned to respect Roman military power, they felt culturally superior. But one of Rome's rare contributions to Greek culture was adding gladiator and wild animal shows to the Olympics until Emperor Constantine (r. 306–337 CE) outlawed the gory shows.[15]

Most Greeks did not become Roman citizens until 212 CE when Rome extended citizenship to all free adult males in the empire under the *Constitutio Antoniniana.* Until then, Greece and some of the past Hellenistic empires, such as Egypt, continued to follow Greek law rather than Roman law. Greek architecture persisted throughout the Roman period. For instance, the outer courts of Herod's temple in Jerusalem were Corinthian in style, although the inner sanctuary followed the Torah's stipulations.[16] Buildings in Rome and throughout the empire followed the classical Greece style but with some new innovations.

Several Asian and North African religions spread throughout the Hellenistic world and later impacted the Roman Empire. In the Hellenistic age, some Greeks had begun worshiping Isis, the Egyptian goddess of fertility, motherhood, and healing, and the cult now spread throughout the Greco-Roman world. The Greeks associated the ancient Vedic god Mithra (Mithras, Mitra), worshiped by the Hindus and Persians, with Helios and Apollo. But the Romans converted this deity's worship into a clandestine cult, where initiates met secretly in caves. Judaism spread; Jewish synagogues (a Greek word meaning "gathering") were scattered in major cities throughout the Greek world.

Within the Greco-Roman milieu, a new religion launched around 30 CE. The Greeks' first contact with Christianity was at its inception. Jesus was born in Judea, which had been part of the Greek world for over three centuries since Alexander the Great conquered the land and was greeted by the Jewish priests at the

---

[15] A. H. M. Jones, "The Greeks under the Roman Empire," *Dumbarton Oaks Papers* 17 (1963): 1–9. https://doi.org/10.2307/1291187.

[16] Jones, "The Greeks under the Roman Empire," 10.

gates of Jerusalem. The Talmud records that Jewish High Priest Shimon HaTzaddik petitioned Alexander the Great to preserve the temple, and Alexander granted their request.[17]

The Judaeans spoke both Koine Greek and Aramaic. When Jesus read from the scroll of Isaiah in the synagogue (Luke 4:17-21), it was the LXX (Koine Greek Septuagint translation), not the Hebrew Tanakh.[18] Jesus and his apostles quoted from this Greek translation more often than the Hebrew version, and the apostles wrote the New Testament in Koine Greek. Apostle John began his Gospel with "Εν ἀρχῇ ἦν ὁ Λόγος" ("In the beginning was the *Logos*"),[19] which had special meaning to the Greeks. The Greek philosopher Heraclitus said the Logos was the invisible fire that drives the systems of the universe. Leucippus said the Logos controlled the movement of atoms. Stoic philosophy taught that the Logos was the universal, divine reason from which life and order proceed.

Apostle John mentioned Greek converts to Judaism who traveled to Jerusalem for the Passover celebration, requesting an audience with Jesus.[20] The Greek-speaking Apostles Paul, Barnabas, Silas, Luke, and Timothy took Christianity to the Greek city-states in Asia, mainland Greece, and Macedonia.[21] When Paul arrived in Athens, he debated with the Epicurean and Stoic philosophers, quoting from the Greek poem *Phaenomena* by Aratus. "In him, we live and move and have our being ... we are his offspring."[22]

---

[17] Yoma 69a, *The William Davidson Talmud (Koren - Steinsaltz)*. https://www.sefaria.org/Yoma.69a.14?lang=bi&with=all&lang2=en

[18] Luke 4:18, "Commentaries," *Bible Hub*. https://biblehub.com/commentaries/luke/4-18.htm

[19] John 1:1, "Interlinear Bible," *Bible Hub*. https://biblehub.com/interlinear/john/1-1.htm

[20] John 12:20-21

[21] Acts 13-17

[22] Acts 17:18-33

Paul in Athens in the Catholic Basilica of St. Dionysius the Areopagite. Paul was not one of the original Twelve Apostles, but he is called an apostle for this importance in early Christianity.

Paul and his cohorts received a mixed reaction from the Greeks. Some were interested and wanted to hear more. Others laughed in contempt. Dionysius, a magistrate in the Areopagus Court, converted and became the first bishop of Athens.[23] In Ephesus, so many people converted from Greek polytheism to Christianity that the silversmiths lost business selling cult images, so they stirred up a mob against Paul.[24] In Cyprus, the Roman proconsul Quintus Sergius Paulus converted.[25] In Macedonia, a wealthy female merchant named Lydia converted.[26]

Within Paul's lifetime, Christian churches sprang up throughout the major cities of the Greek world. Ten books of the New Testament are letters written by Paul to Greek churches or Greek bishops, in which he quoted the Greek philosophers Epimenides and Menander.[27] Some Christians died as martyrs since they were considered an affront to traditional Greek beliefs. In 60 BCE, Apostle Andrew, brother of Simon Peter, was crucified in Patras. Barnabas was stoned to death in Salamis.

The Apostolic Age, the first generation of Christianity, was followed by the ante-Nicene period, which began in 100 CE and continued until 325 CE when the First Council of Nicaea met. Christians experienced several periods of intense persecution by local leaders and various emperors, especially Nero (r. 54–68 CE), Valerian (r. 253–260 CE), and Diocletian (r. 284–305). The Romans considered Christianity a socially divisive cult because the monotheistic Christians refused to bow to the Greco-Roman pantheon of gods or acknowledge the Roman emperor as a deity. The Jews were likewise monotheistic, but their religion was so ancient they were generally tolerated.

Quadratus, the bishop of Athens, was a disciple of the original apostles. When Emperor Hadrian visited Athens in 124 CE, Quadratus presented an explanation of Christianity. Hadrian responded with a favorable proclamation, stating that Christians could not be persecuted merely for being Christian but only if they did something illegal. However, after Hadrian's death, persecution

---

[23] Acts 17:32-34
[24] Acts 19
[25] Acts 13:6-12
[26] Acts 16:11-15
[27] Titus 1:12, 1 Corinthians 15:33

emerged again in some regions of the Roman Empire. Polycarp of Smyrna, who had been schooled by John the Apostle, refused to burn incense in worship of the emperor and was burned at the stake around 156 CE. Despite persecution, about 10 percent of the empire's population was Christian by 300 CE.

Roman Emperor Diocletian divided the empire's leadership into a tetrarchy (four co-rulers) under his authority. He moved his capital from Rome to Nicomedia (in today's Turkey) and ruled western Turkey, Syria, Palestine, and Egypt. Constantius administered Britain and Gaul, Maximum governed Spain, Italy, and Africa's northwestern coast, and Galerius controlled Greece and the rest of the Balkan Peninsula.

When Diocletian fell seriously ill, Galerius pushed him out of the tetrarchy, making himself the lead ruler. He passed the Edict of Toleration in 311 CE, ending Diocletian's great persecution of Christians. Torture and death had done nothing to deter Christianity, which continued growing in vitality and numbers. By 313 CE, the tetrarchy had crumbled, with two emperors left: Constantine (the son of Constantius) and Licinius (a close friend of Galerius). They jointly passed the Edict of Milan, granting Christians and everyone else the freedom to follow the religion of their choice.

The uneasy truce between the two remaining emperors crumbled in 321 CE, and a series of battles ensued. In 324 CE, Constantine defeated Licinius's navy and land army but spared his life, allowing him to live as a private citizen in Thessalonica. After Licinius reportedly tried to stir up support from the Goths in a ploy to regain power, Constantine had Licinius hanged, making himself the sole emperor of the East and West. Constantine rebuilt the ancient Greek colony of Byzantium, where Asia and Europe meet at the Bosphorus Strait, renaming it Constantinople. His new capital represented the union of the East and West.

Constantine called the Eastern and Western church leaders together in Nicaea to iron out the doctrine of the Holy Trinity. Arius, a priest in Alexandria, Egypt, had been teaching that Jesus' existence began at his birth, making him unequal to God the Father, who was infinite. However, most priests held to the Gospel of John, which made it clear that the Logos was with God in the beginning and the creator of all things.[28] The First Council of Nicaea formed the Nicene Creed, which is still used in different forms in many Christian churches:

"I believe ... in one Lord Jesus Christ, the only-begotten Son of God, begotten of the Father before all ages; Light of Light, true God of true God, begotten, not created, of one essence with the Father through Whom all things were made."

After Emperor Constantine died, the Roman Empire went through a period of instability. In 364 CE, Valentinian became emperor, ruling the Western Roman Empire from Milan, Italy, and appointing his brother Valens to rule over the Eastern Roman Empire. He ruled from Constantinople. Valentinian died suddenly of a stroke amid an angry tirade, and his two sons inherited the Western Roman Empire while Valens continued to rule the East. Soon, Valens would confront his greatest nemesis: the Goths, a nomadic Germanic tribe.

The Greek world's history of fending off Indo-European tribes crossing the Alps and moving into southern Europe stretched back for centuries. Celtic-speaking tribes had taken advantage of the destabilization caused by Alexander the Great's untimely death, penetrating Thrace, Illyria, Macedon, and the region around the Black Sea. Ptolemy Ceraunus, the son of Egypt's first Macedonian pharaoh, had seized Macedon's throne, but the Celts killed him, mounting his head on a spear in 279 BCE.

Led by King Brennus, eighty thousand Celtic-speaking Gauls invaded Greece in 279 BCE, targeting the treasures at Delphi's Temple of Apollo. A Greek coalition force led by Athenian General Calippus rushed to defend the sacred land, a holy sanctuary for all Greeks. In a savage battle at Delphi, Brennus committed suicide after being wounded, and the Greeks chased the Gauls out of Greece. The Gallic survivors settled in today's western Turkey, establishing the Kingdom of Galatia.

---

[28] John 1:1-5

The Dying Gaul is a Roman copy of a Greek original.
BeBo86, CC BY-SA 3.0 <https://creativecommons.org/licenses/by-sa/3.0>, via Wikimedia Commons; https://commons.wikimedia.org/wiki/File:Dying_Gaul.jpg

Germanic-speaking tribes also began migrating east and south, reaching the Balkans before 200 BCE. But the Antigonid dynasty of Macedonia (descendants of Antiochus the Great's son Demetrius) barred them from crossing the southern Danube. Centuries later, one tribe called the Heruli migrated to the Black Sea, sailing along its northern shoreline and attacking and conquering its Greek city-states.

In 267 CE, the Heruli ships sailed to southern Greece's Peloponnese Peninsula, raiding Sparta, Corinth, Argos, and Olympia. Heading to the Attica Peninsula, they sacked Athens, destroying the temples, library, and courthouse in the Agora. However, the Heruli left the residential areas in the north and southwest of Athens intact and seemed only interested in looting, not settling in Greece.[29]

---

[29] Lamprini Chioti, "The Herulian Invasion in Athens (267 CE): The Archaeological Evidence," *Destructions, Survival, and Recovery in Ancient Greece* (American School of Classical Studies at Athens: May 16, 2019). https://www.academia.edu/39196609/The_Herulian_invasion_in_Athens_267_CE_The_Archaeological_Evidence

A century later, the Eastern Emperor Valens marched his army to Thrace, facing off against ten thousand Germanic Goths. The Goths killed Valens in the 378 CE Battle of Adrianople, and the catastrophic war obliterated two-thirds of the Eastern Roman Empire's military, including most of its commanders. The Western emperor appointed Theodosius I, the son of a war hero, as the Eastern Roman Empire's new emperor. Rather than fighting the Goths, Theodosius permitted them to settle in the empire and hired them as mercenaries.

Greece's Olympic Games had always been a religious festival to Zeus, with the ritual slaughter of one hundred oxen at the Temple of Zeus followed by a riotous barbeque. The Roman emperors supported the Olympics; Nero even added musical and acting contests to the repertoire and joined the contests. Of course, he won every competition he entered, even a chariot race where he fell out of his chariot and failed to finish. But to discourage traditional Greek polytheism, Theodosius banned animal sacrifices, which put a damper on the Olympic festivities. Nevertheless, the games continued for a few more years until the reign of Theodosius II (402–450 CE), who ordered the Temple of Zeus to be burned.

The Western Roman Empire fell apart within decades, unable to fend off the relentless onslaught of Germanic tribes and Central Asia's Huns. While Rome suffered a horrific famine in 410 CE, Alaric, king of the western Goths, sacked the city. In 455, the Vandals, another Germanic tribe, sacked Rome again. In 475, the eastern Goths forced the Western emperor to abdicate, and the Western Roman Empire collapsed.

Greece and the rest of the Eastern Roman Empire continued until the Ottoman Empire completed the conquest of the Byzantine Empire in 1453 CE. Modern historians refer to the Eastern Roman Empire as the Byzantine Empire after its capital Byzantium (renamed Constantinople). The Byzantine Empire reigned for over a millennium and was a cultural, economic, and military powerhouse. With borders that receded and advanced, it also ruled Egypt, Turkey, and the western Mediterranean coastal areas for some of the time it was in power.

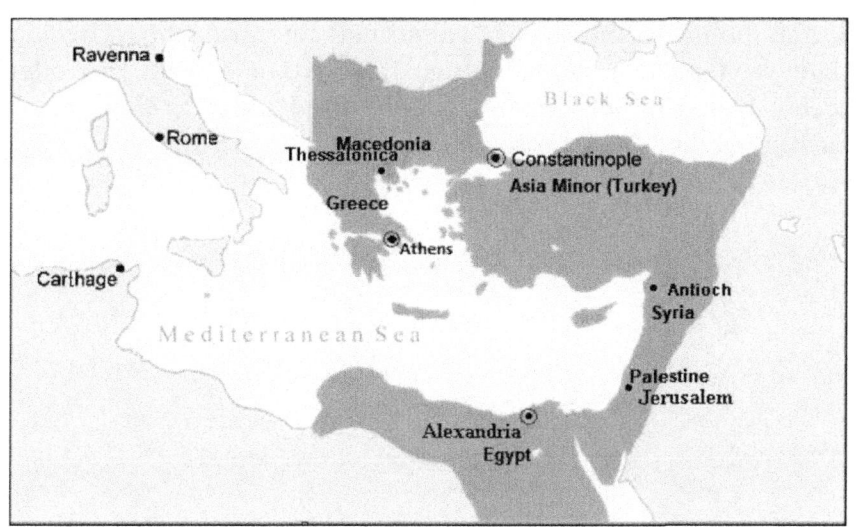

The Byzantine Empire in 476 CE.
Photo modified: labels added. Credit: Darylprasad, CC BY-SA 4.0
<https://creativecommons.org/licenses/by-sa/4.0>, via Wikimedia Commons;
https://commons.wikimedia.org/wiki/File:Byzantium476.png

In 529 CE, Emperor Justinian I revised Roman law into the Justinian Code, which shaped the Byzantine legal system for nine centuries and even influenced modern Greece's laws. It made Christianity the state religion and a requirement for citizenship. Hellenistic culture was still strong in the Byzantine Empire, with Greek philosophy shaping Christian theology. However, the emperors suppressed polytheism. In 529, Justinian I cut state funding for the Neoplatonic Academy, a revival of Plato's original school, which the Roman dictator Sulla destroyed in 86 BCE. The academy's scholars carried their scrolls of philosophy, literature, and science to Ctesiphon in today's Iraq, continuing for another century through its Sassanian dynasty.

The Greeks and the people of the former Hellenistic empires spoke and wrote in Koine Greek during the Roman era. Latin was the official administrative language for the entire Roman Empire, but in the East, it was mainly used in the military and for some administrative functions. When the Western Roman Empire collapsed, the Byzantine Empire continued using the Greek language as the "lingua franca," or common language. Emperor Heraclius (r. 610–641 CE) made Greek the official language of the Byzantine Empire and the only language for governmental affairs.

By this point, Koine Greek had segued into Byzantine Greek or Medieval Greek, a stepping-stone from Koine Greek to Modern Greek. Koine Greek continues to be used today as the liturgical language of the Greek Orthodox Church.

Chapter 8: Byzantium under Greek Influence

The wind rippled through Heraclius's hair as he stood near his ship's bow, to which he had attached an image of the Virgin Mary. Observing Constantinople's skyline from the sea, he could see the Hagia Sofia's dome and the palace, now occupied by the incompetent tyrant Phocas. As his fleet approached, the people of Constantinople immediately overthrew their oppressive ruler, who had tortured and executed anyone he considered a threat. The patriarch of Constantinople crowned Heraclius the new emperor, hoping he could rescue the empire from its multiple crises.

As the people handed Phocas over, Heraclius asked, "Is this how you run our empire?"

"Can you do any better?" Phocas bitterly retorted before being hewn into pieces.

Turning the beleaguered Byzantine Empire around was a daunting challenge for Heraclius. Eight years earlier, in 602 CE, Phocas had assassinated Emperor Maurice, killed his wife and three little girls, and usurped the throne. Taking advantage of the chaos in Constantinople, the Persian Sassanid Empire invaded the Byzantine provinces of Armenia and Mesopotamia. By 608, Constantinople's horrified citizens watched the Persians burn villages across the Bosphorus Strait. Meanwhile, the Avar confederation swept into the Balkan Peninsula from today's Ukraine, Russia, and Kazakhstan.

Wreaking havoc in Thrace and northern Greece, they demanded tribute payments from the Byzantine Empire.

Emperor Heraclius's first decade in the war against Persia did not go well. The Persians took Antioch and Damascus, and in 614, they conquered Jerusalem, murdering over fifty thousand citizens, including thousands of nuns and priests. They burned down the city's churches and captured the True Cross, believed to be the one upon which Jesus died. In 618, they invaded Egypt and conquered Alexandria. Egypt was Constantinople's primary grain source, so the city now faced famine.

Heraclius finally launched a successful counteroffensive in 622, marching directly toward Iran and impelling the Persian forces to hurry back to defend their homeland. He overwhelmingly defeated the Persian troops before rushing home to fend off the Avars laying siege to Constantinople. The patriarch rallied the citizens by marching around the wall of Constantinople, carrying an icon of the Virgin Mary. Meanwhile, Heraclius arranged to meet the khan (king) of the Avars in Thrace to discuss a settlement. On his way, Heraclius narrowly escaped an Avar ambush. He threw off his purple robe, tucked his crown under his arm to avoid recognition, and scurried back to the city unharmed.

After successfully defending his capital, Heraclius led his army back to Asia in 627, scoring a crushing victory in the eleven-hour Battle of Nineveh. The disgruntled Persians overthrew their king and crowned his son, who immediately reached out with peace terms. The Byzantine Empire got their Asian and African territories back, and the Persians returned the True Cross.

The Byzantine Empire reigned as one of the world's longest multi-continent empires in a millennium of palace intrigues, wars on multiple fronts, and religious controversies. The people of the empire never called it the Byzantine Empire; in their minds, it was still the Roman Empire. However, the Western Roman Empire had collapsed, and Rome wasn't within the Eastern Roman Empire's borders, nor did Rome exercise power over the East. Thus, the Renaissance scholars renamed it the Byzantine Empire, although it was a predominantly Greek state culturally. The Byzantine Empire left a rich and lasting legacy of architecture, art, literature, and mystical Eastern Orthodox Christianity. Its imaginative abstract art with spiritual themes reflected the diverse cultures that graced the three-continent empire.

This 6th-century mosaic of Jesus Christ Pantocrator ("all-powerful") in Hagia Sofia reflects the distinctive religious art of the Byzantine Empire.

Edal Anton Lefterov, CC BY-SA 3.0 <https://creativecommons.org/licenses/by-sa/3.0>, via Wikimedia Commons; https://commons.wikimedia.org/wiki/File:Jesus-Christ-from-Hagia-Sophia.jpg

In 610 CE, the same year Heraclius ascended the Byzantine throne, a man in a cave in Arabia was experiencing visions. Muhammad gathered a following and eventually conquered Mecca. While Heraclius was successfully fighting the Persians, Muhammad conquered all of Arabia. After Muhammad died in 632, his impassioned Islamic followers led a holy war to spread their new religion, and the Byzantine Empire was in their crosshairs.

The Muslims began with raids on the Palestine border, which was nothing new. Yet, Heraclius took the threat seriously and remained in Asia. But his age and failing health prevented him from personally commanding his troops. The zealous Muslim troops took Palestine, Transjordan, Syria, and Egypt. Heraclius pulled back and fortified Anatolia (Turkey) against the Islamic tide while the Arabs turned east and crushed the Persian Sassanid Empire.

By Heraclius's death in 641, the Byzantine Empire had lost all of Asia except Anatolia but still held North Africa west of Egypt. Spain was lost, but the Byzantine Empire held the ancient Greek colonies in southern Italy and the islands throughout the Mediterranean. The empire ruled the coastal regions of Greece and the other Balkan territories, but the Avars and Slavs controlled a vast swathe of the central Balkan Peninsula.

Surprisingly, although massively outnumbered by the Arab caliphate forces, the Byzantine Empire kept it from taking more territory. Heraclius's grandson, Constans II, restructured the army, spreading them into units throughout the empire. Instead of receiving a salary, the soldiers received farmland parceled out from former imperial estates. During the next three centuries, the Byzantine Empire recovered its Balkan territories, doubled in population, and became fantastically rich and powerful. In awe, the Russians, Serbs, and Armenians converted to Eastern Orthodox Christianity.[30]

Despite calling itself "Roman" and ruling from a city at the intersection of Europe and Asia, the Byzantine Empire transformed into a culturally Hellenistic power through the spread of the Greek language and culture. Hellenistic art, architecture, literature, theater, and language surged forward in the Byzantine Renaissance, which lasted from the 9th to 11th centuries. Scholars studied Plato and other ancient Greek philosophers, incorporating their ideas into Christian theology.

Anna Komnene, a medical doctor, hospital administrator, and daughter of the 12th-century Emperor Alexios I Komnenos, wrote

---

[30] Warren Treadgold, "The Persistence of Byzantium," *The Wilson Quarterly* 22, no. 4 (1998): 76-7. http://www.jstor.org/stable/40260386.

the *Alexiad*, chronicling the First Crusade. Thoroughly educated in Greek classics, sciences, and rhetoric, she wrote her history in Athens's Attic Greek dialect with an epic poetry style reflecting Homer and Xenophon. The work conveyed the alarm in Constantinople generated by the western European Crusaders marching through the Byzantine Empire on their way to emancipate Jerusalem.[31]

By embracing Hellenistic culture, the Byzantine Empire played an integral role in preserving classical Greek philosophy, literature, and art. Greek culture shaped the Byzantine Empire, which, in turn, transmitted Greek culture to western Europe and the Islamic world.[32] Greek colonists in the archaic and classical eras strongly influenced the region over which the Roman Empire ruled. Later, Alexander the Great and his successors' Hellenistic empires left their stamp on eastern Europe, western Asia, and North Africa. As Rome's importance faded, the Hellenistic cities of Antioch, Alexandria, and Pergamum rose to ascendency as cultural centers.

Despite the inherent incompatibility of Greek polytheism with monotheistic Christianity, the Byzantine Empire fused Hellenistic culture with the Eastern Orthodox Church. They did so cautiously. For instance, the 4th-century Bishop Basil of Caesarea encouraged his students to explore Greek literature and philosophy but to reject anything contradictory to Christianity. Christian theologians found parallels between Plato's ethics and philosophy and the teachings of Christ.[33]

Byzantine monks, like the 15th-century Bessarion who studied Neoplatonism in Greece, copied and preserved the texts of ancient Greek philosophers. Bessarion translated Aristotle's *Metaphysics* and Xenophon's *Memorabilia* and attempted to reconcile Plato and

[31] Romilly J. H. Jenkins, "The Hellenistic Origins of Byzantine Literature," *Dumbarton Oaks Papers* 17 (1963): 37–52. https://doi.org/10.2307/1291189.

[32] Anthony Kaldellis, *Hellenism in Byzantium: The Transformations of Greek Identity and the Reception of the Classical Tradition*, (Cambridge: Cambridge University Press, 2007), 11.

[33] Rakesh Mittal, *Hellenism and the Shaping of the Byzantine Empire*, Marquette University, 2010. https://epublications.marquette.edu/cgi/viewcontent.cgi?article=1001&context=jablonowski_award

Aristotle with Christianity. Students in the Byzantine Empire studied Homer as the founder of literature and received tutoring in Greek rhetoric and philosophy, which were considered essential to a well-rounded education.

Byzantine literature represented a continuation of ancient Greek tradition, replicating the literary styles of Lucian, Homer, and Herodotus. The Byzantine monks who collected, translated, copied, and studied the Greek language and literature safeguarded these extraordinary works well into the Renaissance era. These preserved works impacted Renaissance thinkers and revolutionary politics centuries later.

In *Dialectica*, the 8th-century monk John of Damascus commented on Aristotle's *Prior Analytics*, which deals with deductive reasoning. John's work employed Greek logic to deal with controversies rocking the church regarding the nature of Christ. Aristotle taught that if certain principles are known to be factual, we can make deductions from that. John of Damascus used this deductive process to tackle theological arguments.

Classical Greek scholar and Arab-Christian monk John of Damascus.
https://commons.wikimedia.org/wiki/File:John-of-Damascus_01.jpg

The 9th-century Photius, Patriarch of Constantinople, wrote *Amphilochia*, which included a commentary on Aristotle's *Categories* and his concept of substance and theory of predication. The 11th-century monk and savant Michael Psellos reintroduced the study of Plato and wrote *De Omnifaria Doctrina*, which deals with Aristotle's *Categories* and *Prior Analytics*. Psellos was so engrossed in Greek philosophy that his friends began to doubt his Christian faith.

In the early Byzantine Empire, the only cities with a population of over 100,000 were Alexandria, Antioch, and Constantinople. Constantinople was the largest, with around 400,000 at its height. Despite the urban prosperity, about 90 percent of the Byzantine Empire's population were illiterate rural farmers scratching out a living, which was typical of medieval society. Even so, throughout most of its history, the Byzantine Empire outshone western Europe with its efficient government and diversified economy.[34]

How did the Byzantine Empire survive almost a thousand years after the Western Roman Empire fell? One reason was economics. The Western Roman Empire enriched itself through conquests, but once it stopped gaining additional territory, the flow of wealth slowed to a trickle. Although the Byzantine Empire gained some wealth from conquering the Persian Empire, the costs involved in the decades-long war blunted its impact. The Byzantine Empire's economy centered around sea trade. The Greeks had traded and colonized around the Mediterranean, Aegean, and Black Seas since the archaic era, and their vast sea trade continued with the Byzantine Empire.

Ancient Troy had once grown unimaginably wealthy by reigning over the straits linking the Aegean and Black Seas. Constantinople's strategic location likewise gave it control of ship traffic between the two seas. The other two major cities—Alexandria and Antioch—were situated for profitable sea trade in the Mediterranean. Alexandria lay on a branch of the Nile that emptied into the sea. Antioch, Syria, was on an island in the Orontes River close to the Mediterranean. After Antioch fell to the Arabs in 637 CE and Alexandria in 641,

---

[34]Treadgold, "The Persistence of Byzantium," 69-70.

Thessaloniki in northern Greece on the Aegean Sea rose in prominence, becoming the empire's second-largest city.

The city of Constantine lay on a triangular-shaped peninsula surrounded on three sides by water. The Sea of Marmara was to the south, the Golden Horn waterway to the north, the Bosphorus Strait to the east, and Greece and Thrace (Bulgaria) to the west. The Bosphorus connected the Black Sea to the Aegean Sea and was the boundary line between Europe and Asia. Constantinople's location positioned it for wealthy sea trade and lucrative intercontinental land trade.

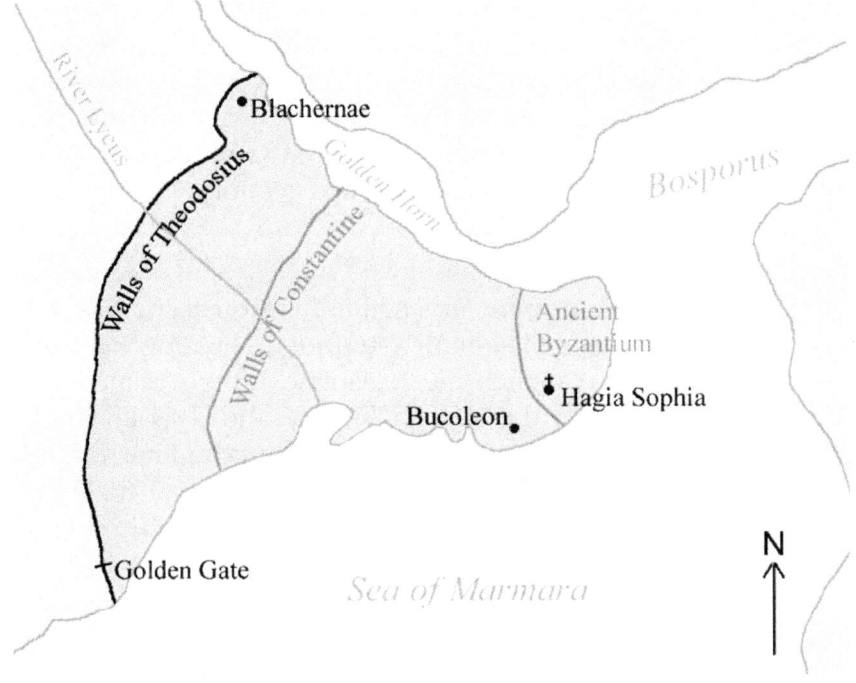

Constantinople (today's Istanbul) was the capital of the Byzantine Empire.
Jniemenmaa, CC BY-SA 3.0 <http://creativecommons.org/licenses/by-sa/3.0/>, via Wikimedia Commons; https://commons.wikimedia.org/wiki/File:Constantinople.png

When Constantine enlarged and transformed the ancient Greek city of Byzantium into Constantinople, he built a new wall. It stretched from the Sea of Marmara to the Golden Horn estuary, protecting the city from invasion by land. He brought priceless art pieces and sculptures from Rome. Constantine needed people to fill his lavish new city, so he enticed noblemen with land grants and free food for the working class.

The Byzantine emperor technically had almost unlimited power. Still, he needed the acknowledgment and favor of his citizens and the patriarch of Constantinople. If he became a tyrannical despot, he risked being overthrown, which happened to Andronicus I Komnenos in 1185 CE after a two-year rule. The church expected the emperors to comply with its moral standards. Although none came close, the patriarch of Constantinople wasn't as likely to excuse them as the Roman pope. Some Byzantine religious artwork showed emperors burning in hell.[35]

Like in Rome, the Byzantine emperors worked with a senate. Unlike Rome, the senators were not from the elite class but military men who had worked their way through the ranks. The Byzantine government followed the rule of law, but the emperor could change the laws. Despite being hierarchal, a fascinating aspect of Byzantine society was that it allowed for upward mobility. A prostitute could become an empress, like Justinian I's wife Theodora, and an uneducated peasant could become an emperor, like Basil I.

Basil's skills in winning wrestling matches and taming unruly horses caught the attention of Emperor Michael III. The emperor made Basil his bodyguard and confidant, then had him marry his mistress Eudokia, who was pregnant with Michael's son Leo. When Leo was born in 866 CE, Michael made Basil his junior co-emperor so that his son with Eudokia would be of "legitimate" royal birth. The whole affair backfired on Michael when Basil assassinated him the following year. As junior emperor, Basil automatically ascended the throne. Amazingly, he was a competent emperor. He reconquered the ancient Greek city-states of southern Italy, trounced the Arab caliphate, and rewrote the legal code of the Byzantine Empire.

The Greek Orthodox Church, as it was known after its 11th-century schism from Rome, profoundly influenced the Byzantine Empire's government and culture. It was called the "Greek" Orthodox Church then, not because it was only in Greece or for Greek people but because Koine Greek was the liturgical language. Today, the name "Greek Orthodox Church" refers to the

---

[35] Treadgold, "The Persistence of Byzantium," 70-71.

Orthodox churches in Greece or among Greek people worldwide and is part of the larger Eastern Orthodox Church (or Orthodox Catholic Church).

The Byzantine emperor appointed the patriarch (a major archbishop) of Constantinople and had the authority to remove him. Beginning in the 4th century, the patriarch of Constantinople held the second place of honor among archbishops after the pope in Rome. The Byzantine church was known for its monasticism, where men and women, often from the nobility, abandoned their luxurious lives to live as ascetics in monasteries and convents.

This mosaic of Empress Theodora, wife of Justinian I, is in the Basilica of San Vitale (built 547 CE) in Ravenna, Italy.

The monastics devoted themselves to communal worship and scholarly pursuits in the monasteries' libraries of ancient texts. The monks and nuns also cared for orphans, the elderly, the needy, and the sick. Empress Theodora, the wife of Emperor Justinian I (r. 527–565), had been a prostitute before her marriage. After becoming empress, she bought and emancipated girls sold into prostitution, sending them to a convent she established so they could learn a trade to support themselves.

A fierce controversy that rocked the Orthodox Church, especially in the 8th century CE, was the question of icons: images of Jesus, the Virgin Mary, and the saints. These statues and paintings had been an integral part of worship in Rome and the Eastern Orthodox Church. But Emperor Leo III and others felt that icons were essentially idols and banned them in 730. Fifty-seven years later, Empress Irene became the de facto ruler as regent for her ten-year-old son. She organized the Seventh Ecumenical Council at Nicaea, which made icons legal again. The decision was overturned in 815, but Empress Theodora, the widow of Emperor Theophilus, restored the veneration of images in 843.

Hagia Sophia was completed in 537 CE. The Ottomans added the minarets.
Photo zoomed in. Credit: Dennis Jarvis from Halifax, Canada, CC BY-SA 2.0
<https://creativecommons.org/licenses/by-sa/2.0>, via Wikimedia Commons
https://commons.wikimedia.org/wiki/File:Turkey-3019_-_Hagia_Sophia_(2216460729).jpg

Isadore of Miletus, a brilliant Greek architect and scientist, and Anthemius, another Greek architect and master of Euclidean geometry, designed the Hagia Sofia Cathedral. Commissioned by Emperor Justinian I and completed in 537 CE, Hagia Sofia (the Church of Holy Wisdom) was the world's largest cathedral for almost a thousand years. An earthquake damaged the dome in 558, and Isadore's nephew rebuilt it, making it higher and more resilient to earthquakes. When the Ottomans conquered Constantinople in 1453, they converted it into a mosque. The 6th-century Hagia Sofia still graces Istanbul today.

Chapter 9: Last Years of Byzantium

"Theodora! I haven't much longer to live, and we need to get the succession sorted out." Constantine VIII rose on one elbow on his bed. "I haven't any sons, so you must marry Romanos Argyros. That's the only way he'll be accepted as the new emperor."

"I cannot marry Romanos!" Theodora paced back and forth in agitation.

"Why not? You'll be the new empress!"

"Father! He's married! At least he was until you forced him to divorce his wife and send her to a nunnery! I will not bring God's judgment down on myself by marrying him. Besides, Romanos is my cousin! We're too closely related to marry."

"Oh, Theodora!" Constantine sighed and fell back on his pillow. "Go back to your religious devotion, and send your sister to me. I'll see if Zoe will marry Romanos."

Theodora's sister Zoe did marry Romanos, and Constantine died the next day, making the couple the new emperor and empress in 1028. Theodora escaped the palace drama by sequestering herself in a monastery. After six years, unhappy in her marriage, Zoe and her young lover Michael drowned Romanos in his bath and married each other the same day. They bribed the patriarch of Constantinople to crown Michael as the new emperor and adopted

Michael's nephew, Michael Kalaphates, since they had no child to inherit the throne.

When Emperor Michael died six years later, Michael Kalaphates became emperor and banished Zoe to a monastery. But the people of Constantinople revolted, sending Michael off into exile. They retrieved both Theodora and Zoe from their respective monasteries. And that was how the Byzantine Empire came to be ruled by two empresses, not as regents or wives but in their own right.

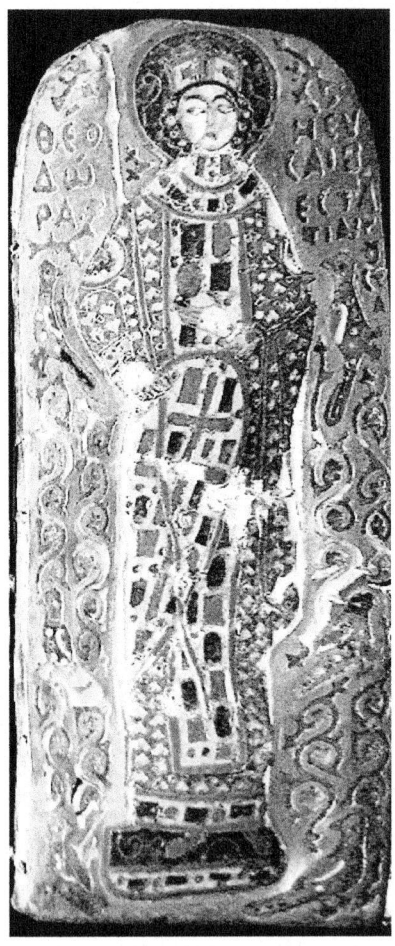

Theodora Porphyrogenita was co-empress with her sister Zoe and then ruled as sole emperor.
https://commons.wikimedia.org/wiki/File:Theodora_Porphyrogenita_in_the_Monomachu s_Crown_(2).jpg

Although outraged at being forcibly removed from her beloved monastery, Theodora was a diligent empress. Zoe quickly married an old lover, Constantine Monomachos. All three ruled the empire; however, their neglect of the military left the empire vulnerable to the Turco-Persian Seljuk Empire. After Zoe died in 1050 and Constantine in 1055, the imperial guard proclaimed Theodora "emperor." Theodora reigned as the Byzantine Empire's sole emperor for twenty months until her death.

Church history took a dramatic turn during the co-reign of Theodora and her brother-in-law Constantine. Roman Pope Leo III excommunicated the patriarch of Constantinople, Michael Cerularius, in the Great Schism (1054 CE). The Eastern and Western Churches had disputed complicated religious issues for centuries, including how to observe Holy Communion and the precise wording of the Nicene Creed. The Eastern Church thought priests could marry, and the Roman Church believed they should be celibate.

Then, there was the question of who had ultimate power. Pope Nicholas I (in. off. 858–867 CE) claimed his dominion extended over all the earth. Now that Rome was a backwater and Constantinople was the largest and most powerful European city, Constantinople claimed its patriarch was equal to the pope. For one thing, Constantinople was a theocracy, with its emperor acting as the "Viceroy of God" and the "interpreter of the Word of God."[36]

The simmering tensions between Rome and Constantinople reached a boiling point in 1054 when Rome excommunicated Constantinople's Patriarch Michael Cerularius. Constantinople fired back by excommunicating the Roman pope and his representatives in July 1054, although Leo had died three months prior, and a new pope had not yet been selected. Despite attempts to heal the breach, the Christian Church existed as two self-governing factions from this point forward.

Hard on the heels of this crisis followed the 1071 invasion of the Seljuk Turks. The Battle of Manzikert in Anatolia (Turkey) ended

---

[36] Steven Runciman, *The Byzantine Theocracy: The Weil Lectures, Cincinnati* (Cambridge: Cambridge University Press, 2004). ISBN 978-0-521-54591-4.

in catastrophe: the Turks decimated most of the Byzantine Empire's professional troops and captured Emperor Romanos IV Diogenes. Sultan Alp Arslan of the Seljuk Empire pushed the emperor's neck to the ground with his foot.

"What would you do if I were in your place?" the sultan asked.

"Maybe kill you. Or parade you through the streets of Constantinople."

The sultan smiled. "I'm giving you a heavier punishment. I'm forgiving you and setting you free."[37]

For the next week, Romanos dined with Alp Arslan while they hashed out terms of surrender. Romanos agreed to pay 1.5 million gold pieces in ransom and an annual tribute of 360,000 gold pieces. The emperor offered his daughter in marriage to the sultan's son, and the sultan provided safe passage back to Constantinople. Things weren't so rosy back home. The Doukas family had staged a coup; they captured Romanos when he returned and gouged out his eyes. Romanos died from the infected wounds shortly after.

Two decades later, the First Crusade set out from western Europe to retake Jerusalem and other holy sites from Islamic control. Although it still lagged behind the Byzantine Empire, western Europe was recovering from its Dark Ages, which saw an economic and cultural decline following the fall of the Western Roman Empire. The Byzantine Empire had lost many territories in Anatolia, Syria, and Palestine to the Seljuk Turks, so Emperor Alexios Komnenos reached out to Pope Urban II for help.

Forty years had passed since the Great Schism, and the strained relationship between the Greek Orthodox Church and the Roman Catholic Church continued. Yet both the Eastern and Western Churches were disturbed that the Seljuk Turks, who had converted to Sunni Islam a century earlier, now controlled the Holy Land. And not just the Holy Land; the Seljuk Empire stretched from the Hindu Kush mountain range of Afghanistan to the Mediterranean and from the Black Sea in the north to the Persian Gulf. Emperor Alexios wanted the empire's lost lands back and to protect the

[37] R. Scott Peoples, *Crusade of Kings* (Rockville, MD: Wildside Press LLC, 2013), 13. ISBN 978-0-8095-7221-2

European side of the empire from the Turks.

Pope Urban II thought that assisting the Byzantine Empire and retaking the Holy Land might reunite the two churches with him at the helm. In 1095, he rallied Christians in Europe to march east to defend the Byzantines from the Turks and retake Jerusalem. Ordinary citizens and professional armies, stirred with religious zeal, marched through the Byzantine Empire toward Constantinople in 1096, their launching point for Asia. While appreciative of their help in retaking the Byzantine Empire's former territory, Byzantine Emperor Alexios and his people were unnerved by the tens of thousands of armed western Europeans gathering in their capital city. Moreover, the soldiers had freely scavenged from farms as they passed through Byzantine lands.

A 13ᵗʰ-century depiction of Godfrey of Bouillon leading the First Crusade.

Alexios required all Crusaders to swear loyalty to him, confirming that the Crusaders would return any former Byzantine territory they recouped to his empire. Alexios did not command the western forces, nor did many Byzantines join in, but the empire provided logistical support. The soldiers of the First Crusade (1095–1099) recaptured the ancient Greek cities of Nicaea, Edessa, and Antioch. Finally, in 1099, they retook Jerusalem, slaughtering thousands of Muslims in the process.

Almost fifty years later, the Second Crusade set out after the Seljuks recaptured Edessa, killing and enslaving its Christian citizens. King Louis VII of France and King Conrad III of Germany led their forces in 1147, but their efforts to retake Edessa and Damascus ended in abject failure. In 1187, Jerusalem fell to Saladin, a Sunni Muslim of Kurdish descent and sultan of Syria and Egypt, sparking Pope Leo III to call for the Third Crusade.

The Crusaders headed east, led by England's King Richard the Lionheart, King Philip II of France, and Holy Roman Emperor Frederick I Barbarossa. King Frederick led his forces out first in 1190 but drowned in a river in Turkey. The French and English arrived by sea in 1191 in time to help a French knight, Guy of Jerusalem, in a successful counterattack against Saladin at Acre in northern Israel. When terms of surrender fell apart, King Richard decapitated 2,700 Muslim prisoners, and Saladin killed all his Christian prisoners. Finally, Richard and Saladin agreed to a treaty that permitted safe passage for Christian pilgrims traveling to the Holy Land.

The Crusades enabled the Byzantine Empire to reclaim most of its holdings along the eastern Aegean coastline, wealthy city-states that had been established by the Greeks two millennia earlier. However, the Byzantine Empire continued to neglect its military, happy to let the western European Crusaders fight on their behalf. The western Europeans passing through Constantinople took note of the city's staggering wealth, weak military, and unstable monarchy.

And then, it happened. Instead of fighting the Turks, the Crusaders turned on the Byzantine Empire and attacked Constantinople. It all started with a series of coup d'états beginning in 1183. Andronikos I Komnenos, who had been seducing princesses throughout Europe and Asia, suddenly turned on his thirteen-year-old cousin, Emperor Alexios II, usurping his throne. Andronikos mercilessly killed the boy, his mother, and thousands of western Europeans living in Constantinople.

Andronikos's chaotic reign ended two years later when Constantinople's citizens revolted. The emperor tried to flee with his wife and mistress (yes, both) by boat, but he was captured, tortured for three days, killed, and left unburied. A distant relative, Isaac II Angelos, became emperor in 1185 and successfully fended off Norman King William II of Sicily, who had invaded the Balkans. When the Third Crusade launched, some of the Crusaders looted Byzantine settlements, an ominous foretaste of what was to come. Nevertheless, Isaac failed to shore up his land forces or naval fleet, which had shrunk to only thirty ships.

In 1195, Isaac's brother, Alexios Angelos, staged a coup. He blinded Isaac, threw him into a dungeon, and usurped the throne. Alexios III emptied the state treasury, passing out bribes to secure his position. He looted the former emperors' tombs and crushed his citizens with heavy taxes. The empire was in dire straits, with the Hungarians, Bulgarians, Romanian Vlachs, and Seljuk Turks launching raids from the north and east.

Isaac II was still in the dungeon, but his son, Alexios IV Angelos, approached the soldiers gathering in Venice for the Fourth Crusade. He struck a deal: if they could make him the empire's new king and get rid of his uncle, Alexios III, he would end the Great Schism with Rome and fund their Crusade. In 1203, the Crusaders besieged Constantinople, burning part of the city. Although Alexios III's men outnumbered the Crusaders, he was afraid to fight and escaped to Thrace.

Constantinople's citizens retrieved Isaac II from the dungeon. They clothed him in purple, but because he was blind, the Crusaders insisted Alexios IV should be the new emperor. Alexios needed to pay off the Crusaders but was horrified to discover that his uncle had emptied the state coffers. He melted down gold and silver icons from the churches but could only meet half the amount he had promised the Crusaders. Enraged at the desecration of their sacred statues, the citizens of Constantinople took to the streets in violent protests. The usurper Doukas Mourtzouphlos took advantage of the chaos and imprisoned and strangled Alexios IV. Isaac II died about the same time, and Mourtzouphlos was crowned Alexios V.

The Crusaders were furious at not receiving the total promised amount of money and at the murder of the king they had installed. Pope Innocent III commanded them *not* to attack Constantinople again, but the priests accompanying the Crusaders ignored his order. In April 1204, the Crusaders sailed across the Bosphorus and sacked Constantinople for three days, looting priceless artwork, raping nuns, and murdering Orthodox priests. They desecrated the Hagia Sofia Cathedral, destroying ancient sacred texts and drinking wine from the Holy Communion vessels.

Following Constantinople's fall, the western Europeans quickly conquered northern Greece, Thessaly, and Thrace. Most of the Greeks in the conquered territories fled to the three states still held by the Byzantines. The "Empire of Nicaea" stretched from the Aegean to the Black Sea. Alexios III's son-in-law, Theodore Lascaris, was crowned in 1205. Nicaea became the new patriarchal seat of the Orthodox Church. The second remaining Byzantine state was the Despotate of Epirus on the Adriatic coast, ruling over northwestern Greece and a section of Thessaly. On the southwestern shore of the Black Sea lay the third state, the Empire of Trebizond, which had been captured by former Emperor Andronicus's grandsons.

In Nicaea, Theodore I immediately faced an attack from Baldwin, the first emperor of what was now Latin Constantinople. Theodore suffered a bitter loss of territory along the Black Sea coastline. However, the Greeks who remained in Thrace struck an alliance with Tsar Kalojan of Bulgaria. In 1205, he attacked Emperor Baldwin's army, capturing the emperor, who died in prison. By 1241, Latin-held territories in the previous Byzantine Empire had shrunk to little more than the city of Constantinople. Emperor John Vatatzes of Nicaea was setting the stage to retake Constantinople. With the Bulgarians distracted by the Mongols sweeping in from Asia, he brought Thessalonica and Epirus under his control.

After Vatatzes's death, his son, Theodore II Lascaris, incompetently continued his quest until he died four years later from epilepsy. A palace coup brought the crown to Michael VIII Palaiologos, who descended from all three of Constantinople's imperial families. He ruled as co-emperor with Theodore's seven-year-old son John IV. In 1261, his general, Alexius Strategopoulos, was heading to Thrace when he learned that the Latin military was away from Constantinople attacking Daphnusia Island (Kefken Island) in the Black Sea. He also learned of a narrow, unguarded gate in Constantinople's walls and sent a small detachment of men through.

They overcame the unsuspecting guards and opened the main gate to Strategopoulos's army, who poured into the unguarded city. Emperor Baldwin and most of the Latins escaped to Euboea. Michael was crowned emperor of Constantinople, but he blinded his co-emperor of Nicaea, John IV, on his eleventh birthday. The patriarch of Constantinople excommunicated Michael for his crime, but blindness eliminated John's ability to rule either Nicaea or Constantinople.

For the next two centuries, Michael's descendants—the Palaiologan dynasty—ruled the restored Byzantine Empire. Initially, they recouped much of the empire's former glory and power, but they repeated some fatal flaws: neglecting their military and engaging in a brutal civil war. This left the empire vulnerable to the Ottoman Turks, who took most of Anatolia by 1305.

In 1348, the Black Death reached the Byzantine Empire: a pandemic of bubonic plague that caused huge lymphatic boils to break out all over the body and ooze bloody pus. People would vomit blood, and their fingers, toes, noses, and lips would turn black with gangrene. The Black Death was the deadliest pandemic in world history and killed up to 90 percent of those infected, sometimes within one day of symptom onset. At least one-third of Europe's population died from the Black Death, even more in the coastal regions. Located between two seas, Constantinople suffered dreadfully, as did the Greek islands and coastal cities.

Finally, the plague burned out, and Constantinople limped along for another century before the Ottoman conquest. In the empire's latter years, ancient Greek philosophy began to reemerge, specifically, Neoplatonic thought. The Byzantine Empire was the world's only postclassical culture that continued to speak and write

Greek, which gave them immediate access to Hellenistic literature. The Byzantine Empire was "a fascinating laboratory for cultural and intellectual fusion, reception, combination, and reinvention."[38]

The Byzantines applied Plato's philosophy to the new political world that was no longer pagan but Christian. They realized that Aristotle, Plato, and other Greek philosophers had rejected the concept of multiple gods who sinned as flagrantly as humans. Texts by Byzantine's Komnenian dynasty used Aristotelian terms to interpret historical conflicts. Byzantine intellectual history contextualized classical Greek thought to fit their milieu, and it continued to shape their worldview. They didn't just use Neoplatonic theory and other Greek philosophies to push their agenda; they were committed to its truth. Hellenism and Christianity weren't necessarily worldviews in tension but parallel discourses.[39]

Constantinople had withstood multiple sieges through the centuries thanks to being surrounded by water on three sides. Three defensive walls and a moat guarded the western side facing land. Yet, the Islamic Ottoman Empire of western Turkey was encroaching on Europe, having already taken Thrace, Serbia, and Thessaloniki. The Byzantines foiled two Ottoman attacks on Constantinople in 1394 and 1422. But in 1453, Sultan Mehmed II blockaded the city, preventing whatever help the western Europeans could lend.

---

[38] Anthony Kaldellis, *Hellenism in Byzantium: The Transformations of Greek Identity and the Reception of the Classical Tradition* (Cambridge: Cambridge University Press, 2007). https://www.cambridge.org/core/books/cambridge-intellectual-history-of-byzantium/introduction/6301574643465C8A8D0D73A01EA92AD1

[39] Kaldellis, *Hellenism in Byzantium*.

A restored section of Constantinople's walls.

Constantinople only had five thousand fighting men and twenty-six ships under the command of Emperor Constantine XI to fend off the massive Ottoman army. They had catapults, but the Turks had even newer technology: the Turkish Bombard, a twenty-seven-foot-long cannon that could launch six-hundred-pound stones. For six weeks, the Ottoman Turks pulverized Constantinople's walls, and on May 29th, 1453, the Ottomans flooded the city, killing Emperor Constantine. They pillaged the city, slaying thousands. They enslaved fifty thousand inhabitants. The Muslims converted the Hagia Sofia Cathedral into a mosque and renamed Constantinople Istanbul, which became the capital of the Ottoman Empire.

But the ancient Greek culture persisted. Some Greek scholars had prudently left when the Ottomans were attacking surrounding regions. Others were able to escape during or immediately after Constantinople's fall. They made their way to Italy with priceless Greek manuscripts from classical philosophers like Plato and Aristotle, which were then translated into Latin. These scholars' knowledge of astronomy, architecture, poetry, music, and political theory helped create the early Renaissance: the rebirth of culture, art, and philosophy in western Europe.

PART FOUR:
New and Modern Greek History (1453 CE–20th Century)

Chapter 10: Ottoman Rule and the War of Independence

"Domenikos! What will we do about the *paidomazoma*? They'll be coming soon!"

"Don't worry so much, Philippa. They might not choose our children."

"They take one in five, Domenikos! The strongest and most handsome boys. They'll take Nicholas! I know they will!"

Domenikos tried to soothe his wife. "It might not be so bad. They'll train him to fight in the elite corps or serve as a civil servant. He would have a chance at a better life."

"Domenikos! They'll force him to become Muslim. What if they castrate him and make him a eunuch? And Agatha! She's growing into a beauty. They'll take her for the harems, and she'll never see the light of day again!"

Domenikos cleared his throat. "If we convert to Islam, they won't take our children. We needn't really convert; we'll become crypto-Christians. In our hearts, we'll follow Christ."

But tears rolled down Philippa's cheeks. "We're forced to choose between our children and our God? I fear for all our souls!"

Greece crumbled, bit by bit, to the Turkish Ottoman Empire within fifty years after Constantinople fell in 1453. For over three centuries, the Greeks suffered brutal atrocities and humiliations under the Ottoman occupation. The Ottomans forced Christian communities to hand over one-fifth of their children as "tribute." They forbade them to carry weapons or travel by horse. If a Christian family converted to Islam and was found secretly practicing Christianity, they were executed. Greece's economy suffered, literacy declined, and its population dwindled.

Sultan Mehmed II and Patriarch Gennadios II.

However, the Muslims allowed the Orthodox Church to continue; they even appointed the patriarchs. Sultan Mehmed II, the twenty-one-year-old who had conquered Constantinople, handed the patriarchal staff to Gennadios Scholarios, his choice for the new ecumenical patriarch. Mehmed declared the patriarch the supreme representative of all Greek Orthodox Christians in the Ottoman Empire. The patriarch was responsible for the Christians' law-abiding behavior and was their highest judicial authority, especially regarding family and inheritance law.[40]

Part of Mehmed's rationale for restoring power to the patriarch was maintaining the schism between the Greek Orthodox Church and the Roman Catholic Church. He didn't want the pope in Rome telling Christians in his empire what to do. And yet, the patriarchate played a pivotal role in shaping modern Hellenism into a cohesive, unified body and carrying on the Greek intellectual tradition. Orthodox priests were now essentially the leaders of Greek communities, controlling the schools and courts.

The Ottoman Empire's ongoing conflict with the Republic of Venice for control of the Aegean, Ionian, and Adriatic Seas began before Constantinople fell. The Turks scored a decisive victory in the 1499 Battle of Zonchio, the first time they used cannons on their ships. In the Ottoman-Venetian War (1537–1540), Sultan Suleyman I allied with France against Holy Roman Emperor Charles V. They planned a simultaneous attack on Italy: France from the north and the Ottomans from the south. But the French got distracted with the Netherlands and didn't make it to Italy. So, the Ottoman forces left Italy, sailed to the Adriatic Sea, and trounced the Holy League alliance of European states in the 1538 Battle of Preveza. The wars with Venice raged for almost two more centuries; the Ottoman Empire won all but one, chipping away at Venetian territory.

Through the years of Ottoman occupation, Greek uprisings and revolts sprang up, often taking advantage of the times the Turks were distracted by their wars with Venice. The Kladas brothers, Epifani and Krokodeilos, fought to take Greece's Peloponnese Peninsula back from the Ottoman Empire in the late 1400s. They allied with the Venetians and won some territory, over which Epifani governed. Krokodeilos continued to lead guerilla attacks on the Turks in the Peloponnese for another eleven years until he was captured and flayed alive.

---

[40] Constantinos Svolopoulos, "The Ecumenical Patriarchate in the Ottoman Empire (1453-1923): Adaptation and Change," *Journal of Modern Hellenism.* 17-18 (2000-2001): 107-110.

Makarios Melissourgos, a bishop in the Peloponnese, conspired with the Spaniards to instigate an insurgency. Spain had joined a coalition promoted by the pope against the Ottoman Empire, which threatened sea trade in the Mediterranean. The 1571 Battle of Lepanto, fought in the Gulf of Patras in western Greece, was an overwhelming (and rare) victory for the coalition forces against the Ottoman Empire. Melissourgos and his family continued to lead rebel raids on the Ottomans in the Peloponnese, but once the western Europeans left the area, they fled to Italy.

The Society of Friends (*Filiki Eteria*) sprang up in Odesa, Ukraine, in 1814 as a secret organization to rid Greece of Ottoman rule and set up an autonomous Greek government. Odesa was an ancient Greek city colonized in the archaic era. Many members were "Phanariotes" from wealthy Greek merchant families in Constantinople and Russia. Other members were political leaders from Greece or Orthodox priests from the extended Greek world. A key leader was Alexander Ypsilantis, born to a noble Greek family in Constantinople that fled to Russia when it was fighting the Turks. Ypsilantis lost his right arm fighting for Russia against Napoleon Bonaparte but devoted himself to recruiting and training fighters and raising funds. He sent fiery letters to Hellenistic centers, drumming up support for Greek independence.

When the Ottoman Turks conquered Greece, the last holdouts fled to the rugged mountains rather than submit to Islamic rule. The Ottomans were never able to root them out, so these *klephts* (independence fighters) were like the Greek version of Robin Hood and his merry men, stealing from Ottoman tax collectors. They survived as bandits, plundering the Turkish settlements for livestock and goods.

Their ranks grew, with those fleeing oppressive poverty or criminal charges joining them, but they had a violent, dark side. They were prone to vendettas. They robbed Greeks as well as Turks and extorted money from Greek communities in return for protection. Sometimes, the Ottomans even hired them as an area's "peacekeepers" or *armatoles*. Eventually, the klephtic bands became the local rulers of Greece's mountainous regions.

Since the Ottoman Empire forbade Greek Christians from bearing arms, the klephts were among the few Greeks who had weapons. More importantly, they had centuries of fighting experience and knew how to use Greece's rugged mountainous terrain to their advantage against the Turks. As nationalistic fervor grew, they launched guerilla raids on the Ottomans, boosting morale among the Greeks. One of their most powerful chieftains was Dimitrios Makris, who had been initiated into the Filiki Eteria and was a leading fighter in the Greek Revolution.

Dimitrios Makris, klepht and Greek freedom fighter.
https://commons.wikimedia.org/wiki/File:Makris_Dimitrios_Greek_Fighter.JPG

But to give the Greek Revolution justice, we should start at the beginning. Through the centuries of Ottoman occupation, the Greeks were mainly in survival mode, giving scant attention to their cultural heritage. However, Greek literature, philosophy, and art sparked the Renaissance in western Europe. This generated the Age of Reason, with new political discourse leading to sweeping changes in Europe and the British colonies in America. In the 18th century, the universal admiration of the ancient Greek culture led to the

Enlightenment among the Greek intelligentsia, encouraging nationalistic fervor. Even non-Greek Europeans began questioning the miserable existence to which the Greeks had been reduced in their homeland.

Inspired by their classical past, the Greek Enlightenment leaders initially disdained their "priest-ridden" Byzantine history. But then, Konstantinos Paparrigopoulos, a history professor at the University of Athens, promoted a continuum of Greek history with links from the archaic era to modern history. Thus, Enlightenment thinkers began to focus on the glories of the Byzantine era and how it preserved and developed classical thought and art.[41]

Turkish occupation and ultra-conservative Greek Orthodox clerics had isolated Greece from western Europe and America's political, scientific, and industrial revolutions. Yet, as early as 800 BCE, the Greeks had colonized the Mediterranean, Aegean, Ionian, and Black Seas. They had always been seafaring traders. In the late 1700s CE, Greek merchants redeveloped a trade empire stretching from the Mediterranean to India, eventually expanding into the world's largest commercial sea empire.[42] Emigrants escaping Greece's political and economic systems began following these trade routes and went farther afield, reaching America by 1800. The Greek Enlightenment movement spread due to this Greek diaspora.

As the Ottoman Empire slid into economic and military decline, the Greek trading class grew increasingly prosperous. Their interactions with the outside world exposed them to new, revolutionary ideas. With the support of the diaspora and wealthy merchants, Greece now had the economic power to fund a war. Russian Empress Catherine the Great (r. 1762–1796) encouraged Greece's nationalistic flames. She hoped to annex the eastern section of the Ottoman Empire, including Constantinople, with a simultaneous attack on the Ottomans from the Russians and Greeks. But when Russia did go to war against the Ottomans in

---

[41] Richard Clogg, *A Concise History of Greece* (Cambridge: Cambridge University Press, 2021), 1-3.

[42] Clogg, *Concise History of Greece*, 4-6.

1768, the Greeks weren't yet ready to launch their own revolution. Yet, Russia's war and the French Revolution of 1789 stoked the fires of Greek revolutionary zeal.

Rigas Feraios was an author and publisher who rallied support from both klephts and Greek Orthodox bishops for the cause of an independent Greece. He wrote and published the patriotic hymn "Thourios," which became an anthem of the revolution, part of which read:

"Shall we dwell in caves, just looking out at the branches,

Leaving from the world into bitter slavery?

Better live one hour in freedom

Than forty years in slavery and prison."

The Greek diaspora that clustered in Odesa (in today's Ukraine) lived in Greek neighborhoods with their own churches, schools, and theaters. Their merchants traded among Greek settlements in the Black Sea and the Mediterranean while recruiting soldiers and supporters for the cause. They used a code. When they greeted someone as "friend," it wasn't just a warm greeting but an indication of belonging to the Filiki Eteria (Society of Friends). The "Great Fair" referred to the revolution, and "market readiness" meant how many soldiers were ready to fight in a given area.[43]

In 1818, the Filiki Eteria moved to Constantinople under the leadership of Panagiotis Sekeris, a wealthy merchant. He helped fund the organization and introduced the small society to the Greek elite in the Ottoman capital. The Eteria recruited "apostles": Greek veterans who had fought on the Russian side against Napoleon. They sent the apostles throughout the Greek lands to recruit and train a military force.

The aristocratic Alexander Ypsilantis took the helm of the Filiki Eteria in 1820, bringing his brothers and friends from the wealthy upper class into the fold. The leaders met in October 1820 to hash out the "Great Plan": how and where to start the war of independence. They first considered beginning the war in the

[43]Mark Mazower, *The Greek Revolution: 1821 and the Making of Modern Europe* (New York: Penguin Press, 2021), 10-11.

Peloponnese on November 15th. Ypsilantis reconsidered and decided to launch the war from across Russia's border in Moldovia and Wallachia in the spring. Although within the Ottoman borders, these lands were semi-autonomous, mostly Christian, and led by Christian governors with no Turkish garrisons. Moldavia's Prince Michael Soutzos was a secret member of the Filiki Eteria.

On February 21st, 1821, Ypsilantis launched the revolution in Galati with the rallying cry, "Fight for faith and the fatherland!" Ypsilantis crossed a tributary of the Danube with 4,500 Greek and eastern European soldiers. They marched to Bucharest in Romania, where Ypsilantis discovered he had overestimated Russian and Romanian support, despite sharing the Orthodox faith. The Ottoman army soon crossed the Danube with thirty thousand troops and fought several battles against Ypsilantis's outnumbered Greek forces.

In Istanbul (formerly Constantinople), the Ottomans responded to the uprisings by forcing Patriarch Gregory V to excommunicate the revolutionaries on Easter Sunday. One week later, Turkish soldiers burst into St. George's Cathedral during Divine Liturgy, dragged the patriarch out, and hanged him at the gate, leaving his body suspended for three days. That same day, the Ottomans began the mass execution of bishops, priests, Greek officials, and Greek merchants in Constantinople and Greece, demolishing churches throughout the empire.

The June 19th Battle of Drăgăşani ended the conflict in Moldovia when the drunken Greek commander Karavias ordered an attack before most Greek forces had arrived on the field. Only 500 cavalry units charged out and quickly retreated just as the Sacred Band of about 350 student volunteers marched out. Only about one-third survived, but their sacrifice spurred the resistance movement in the Peloponnese and central Greece, where the revolt erupted on March 25th.

After the debacle at Drăgăşani, Ypsilantis fled to Austria, where Emperor Francis II placed him under house arrest for seven years. But southern Greece's Peloponnese had already scored a major victory in the May 12th, 1821, Battle of Valtetsi. A Turkish force of five thousand attacked the village of Valtetsi, where several companies of Greek revolutionaries had assembled. The Greeks fought from four tower houses, with 80 to 350 men in each tower.

While the Turks besieged the towers, a Greek force of seven hundred arrived and attacked their flank, holding an advantage over the Ottomans on a steep slope. Another Greek battalion entered near the end of the twenty-four-hour battle, completely turning the tide, and the Greeks routed the Turkish forces. By the end of the year, the Greeks were in firm control of central Greece and the Peloponnese in the south. They declared independence in January 1822.

The Battle of Valtetsi in the Peloponnese was the first decisive Greek victory.
https://commons.wikimedia.org/wiki/File:Anagnostaras_by_Hess.jpg

Europe's conservative heads of state were disturbed by Greece's rebellion, as they preferred to maintain the status quo. However, many Europeans applauded the Greeks' audacity. Pastors and professors reminded everyone of their rich heritage of Greek philosophy, literature, and art. Men from all over Europe, especially

France and Italy, sailed to Greece to fight with the revolutionaries. Greek organizations in the United States sent supplies and funding. Appalled by Patriarch Gregory V's execution, Russia severed diplomatic relations with the Ottoman Empire.

The island of Crete had always resisted Ottoman rule, and once Greece declared independence, Crete also revolted. Muhammad Ali Pasha was the Albanian governor of Egypt (part of the Ottoman Empire), and Sultan Mahmud II offered him Crete if he could bring the Cretans in line and help fight the Greeks. Muhammad Ali sent his son-in-law and thirty warships to subdue Crete. Meanwhile, Cyprus (under Ottoman control) sent shiploads of supplies and one thousand Cypriots to Greece to fight. In July 1821, the Ottomans retaliated by executing Archbishop Kyprianos of Cyprus, three other Cypriot bishops, and all the abbots and monks in Cyprus.

Albanian-speaking islanders from the Aegean Sea manned the Greek revolutionaries' naval fleet, but they usually had merchant ships rather than warships. Since the Ottoman Empire overshadowed them with bigger and better-armed warships, the Greeks resorted to an ancient tactic: fireships. They filled small ships with highly flammable materials. A skeleton crew then steered the vessel toward the Ottoman fleet. At the last moment, they set the ship on fire and escaped on a small boat that was pulled behind them. When the wind or tide was just right, the burning ship would drift into the enemy ships, setting them afire and sometimes exploding. A fireship successfully blew up the Ottoman Empire's flagship, killing Commander Kara Ali and over two thousand people. Sadly, some who died were Greeks captured at Chios being transported to the Turkish slave market.

An internal conflict threatened to derail the Greek Revolution, with a civil war erupting between the guerilla fighters from the mountains and General Theodoros Kolokotronis, the Greek commander-in-chief in the Peloponnese. After two civil wars, Kolokotronis was eventually confirmed as the revolution's commander. Still, the infighting left them vulnerable to the Egyptians, who attacked on behalf of the Ottomans. The Egyptians wreaked havoc in the Peloponnese and captured ancient Athens in 1827.

In April 1827, the Greeks elected Ioannis Kapodistrias as their *kyvernetes* or governor. Meanwhile, the Turkish atrocities, Egypt's interference, and hopes of promoting their own interests in the region finally swayed the British, French, and Russian powers to intervene. After the Turks rejected mediation, the allied forces sailed a naval fleet to Navarino Bay in the Peloponnese on October 20th, 1827. A Turkish and Egyptian naval fleet of seventy-eight ships was moored there, and the Ottomans fired first, which was a suicidal act since the allies had longer-range cannons. They sank all but eight of the Turkish and Egyptian ships. Bonfires and the ringing of church bells spread through Greece as news of the overwhelming victory circulated.

Kapodistrias, Greece's first governor, arrived in January 1828 after touring Europe to drum up support. Four months later, Russia declared war on the Ottoman Empire, forcing it to fight on two fronts. Egypt pulled out of Greece in 1828, and the Greeks swiftly expelled the remaining Ottoman garrisons in the Peloponnese. In December 1828, the British, French, and Russian ambassadors hashed out a protocol for an autonomous Greek state ruled by a king but under the authority of the Ottoman sultan. But the Greeks were unhappy with the proposed borders, and Sultan Mahmud declared he would never grant Greece its independence.

The final clash was the September 1829 Battle of Petra in central Greece. A unified Greek army (rather than guerilla bands) led by Demetrios Ypsilantis (Alexander's younger brother) scored a glorious victory, losing only three men but killing one hundred Turks and eliminating the Turkish military presence in Greece. The Ottomans finally agreed to an autonomous Greek state, but by this time, the British and French insisted on a completely independent Greek state with a king.

In May 1832, Britain, France, and Russia offered the Greek throne to the seventeen-year-old Bavarian prince Otto von Wittelsbach, who descended from two Byzantine royal lines. For the first time in its history, Greece was a united, independent country, with a king ruling the entire land.

Chapter 11: Greece in the 19th Century

As he stood at the HMS *Madagascar's* forecastle, a bead of sweat dripped from Otto's temple, despite the sea breeze. He gazed at the villages dotting the shoreline at the base of rugged mountains as the frigate sailed up the Argolic Gulf toward Nafplio. Forty-two ships accompanying him transported the Bavarian Auxiliary Corps: a three-thousand-man force sent to replace the French allied troops struggling to maintain the peace in Greece.

When Otto was born, his grandfather, Maximilian I, was king of Bavaria. When he was ten, his father, Ludwig I, ascended the throne, and his older brother became crown prince. And now, the Great Powers (Russia, Britain, and France) had offered Otto the newly created throne of Greece. He wasn't their first choice; they had chosen Prince Leopold of Saxe-Coburg and Gotha, but he turned them down because of Greece's instability and poverty. Leopold's reluctance was well-founded; Governor Kapodistrias's assassination in 1831 plunged the country into near-anarchy.

The Great Powers' second choice was Otto, who had distant ancestors from the Byzantine-Greek Komnenos dynasty. No one bothered to check with Greece. Otto wasn't old enough to be king, so a regency council of Bavarian advisors was to rule for the next few years until he turned twenty. He'd never been to Greece, didn't speak the language, and was Roman Catholic, not Greek Orthodox.

He'd heard Greece didn't have beer, so he brought his Bavarian brewmaster.

As the HMS *Madagascar* approached Nafplio, Otto wondered if the Greeks would accept him. Could he do this? Could he lead Greece out of chaos and into greatness? He saw thousands of people crowding the docks, and then a great cheer arose. Otto breathed a sigh of relief. As he disembarked, an excited murmur passed through the crowd at the sight of their handsome, young king. They nodded in approval when he changed his name to the Hellenistic "Othon" and wore Greek clothing, including the fustanella skirt.

Greece's first king: Otto Friedrich Ludwig.
https://commons.wikimedia.org/wiki/File:Otto_of_Greece_litograph.jpg

Otto moved Greece's capital from Nafplio to Athens, but by this point, the ancient city had disintegrated into a village of several hundred houses. He immediately set to work restoring Athens, building universities, gardens, a national library, a palace, and a parliament building. Although Otto constructed hospitals and schools throughout Greece, the people's adoration quickly wore off. His regency council disregarded Greek culture, as it was intent on imposing Bavarian ways and an authoritarian government with no Greeks in key positions. They attempted to suppress the Greek monasteries. And then there were the taxes, which were higher than what the Ottoman Empire had levied.

When Otto turned twenty in 1835, his regency council disbanded, but Bavarians continued to serve in the highest administrative positions. King Otto replaced them with Greek ministers in 1837. When he was twenty-one, Otto traveled back to Bavaria and married the beautiful seventeen-year-old Amalia of Oldenburg. She was Lutheran, but any child born to the couple would be baptized in the Greek Orthodox Church.

Amalie of Oldenburg, Queen of Greece. Painting by Karl Joseph Stieler.
https://commons.wikimedia.org/wiki/File;Joseph_Karl_Stieler_-
Duchess_Marie_Frederike_Amalie_of_Oldenburg,_Queen_of_Greece.jpg

At first, the petite, vibrant, and youthful queen charmed the Greeks with her enthusiastic patriotism regarding her adopted country. She labored tirelessly to improve social conditions. But she and Otto never had any children. Who would rule Greece if their king had no sons? The Greek women whispered, "It must be all that dancing and riding horses that are making her infertile."

Otto faced massive challenges as king. Ottoman rule had impoverished Greece, and the years of revolution plunged it into desperate straits. Its rocky, mountainous terrain with inconsistent rainfall had never provided enough farmland to feed a large population. In the distant past, Greece traded for grain with its former colonies around the Mediterranean and Black Seas. But now, it had little funding or goods to exchange.

Most of the arable land was in the hands of powerful clans like the Mavromichalis family, which had assassinated Greece's governor, Kapodistrias. The Great Powers loaned money for Greece to survive, but in exchange, their three legates in Athens interfered in political affairs. Rather than gradually fading out of the picture, the Great Powers inserted themselves more and more into Greek politics.

The Greeks demanded a constitution and legislature to balance Otto's absolute monarchy. Issues reached a boiling point in 1843, and the heroes from the Greek War of Independence revolted. They insisted on a constitution, the right for all males to vote, and the elimination of Bavarians in the government. After a bloodless coup, Otto granted the Greeks their constitution in 1844, and most Bavarians left. Universal voting rights would have to wait until the next king, though.

The Greeks' next dilemma regarded the Greeks outside their borders. These Greeks lived in lands like Macedonia, Thrace, Epirus, the Aegean Islands, Cyprus, and Crete, which had all been part of the Greek world since ancient times. However, in the mid-1800s, they were still under Ottoman domination. The Greeks' "Great Idea" was to bring all these territories into the Greek state, reviving the Byzantine Empire with Constantinople as its capital.[44]

The Crimean War (1853–1856) erupted when Russia made a power grab for Ottoman territories in the Middle East and the

---

[44] Roumen Daskalov and Tchavdar Marinov, *Entangled Histories of the Balkans - Volume One: National Ideologies and Language Policies.* (Leiden, Brill, 2013), 200.

eastern Mediterranean. Britain, France, Sardinia, and Turkey jumped in against Russia, and the Greeks thought it was an opportune time to retrieve Thessaly and Epirus. But Britain and France stymied their attempts. Russia lost the war, and Greece failed to regain any territory.

The Greeks were dissatisfied with King Otto's authoritarian rule, his dismissal of Prime Minister Konstantinos Kanaris, and his lack of support in invading Thrace and Epirus. When he and the queen visited the Peloponnese in 1862, a rebellion arose, and the Greeks deposed King Otto after a thirty-year reign. In Otto's mind, as he and Amalia boarded a British warship for their voyage to Germany, his exile was not permanent.

Yet, the Greeks were ready for a fresh start and liked Prince Alfred of Britain. However, Queen Victoria had other plans for her second son. Following the Great Powers' recommendation, the Greeks elected a seventeen-year-old prince of Denmark to become their new king: George I. He was the son of Denmark's heir presumptive, Christian IX, who would become the Danish king a few months later. George I was a distant descendant of Emperor Isaac II Angelos of the Byzantine Empire through his mother.

Although George spoke Danish, English, French, and German, he didn't know Greek but quickly mastered the language. His siblings' marriages into European royal families brought him a stellar network of alliances that served Greece well. His sister, Alexandra, married the future King Edward VII of Britain, and his older brother, Frederick, became Denmark's king. Another sister, Dagmar, married the Russian tsar's son, Alexander III, and became Empress Marie in 1881.

In 1863, shortly after George was crowned king of Greece in Copenhagen, Dagmar introduced him to the twelve-year-old Grand Duchess Olga Constantinovna of Russia, whom he married four years later. George was Lutheran, but Olga was an Orthodox Christian, which pleased their Greek subjects. They had eight children together, and their descendants ruled Greece until 1967. Their grandson, Prince Philip, married Princess Elizabeth, later Queen Elizabeth II of England.

George I and Olga with Olga's sister, Grand Duchess Vera Constantinovna of Russia.
https://commons.wikimedia.org/wiki/File:Vera_with_her_sister_Olga_and_brother-in-law_George.jpg

Since he was still a minor, King George traveled to Greece with two Danish advisors: his uncle, Prince Julius, and Count Wilhelm Sponneck. In his first year, he asked the Greek Assembly to write a new constitution, which provided voting rights for all male citizens (the women would have to wait another ninety years). He sent his uncle Julius back to Denmark in his second year when he caught him attempting to remove Sponneck. Sponneck continued to serve as George's advisor for another twelve years, although the Greeks disliked him because of his boorish, ethnocentric attitude. He even questioned whether the modern-day Greeks were descendants of the ancient classical Greeks.

The seven Ionian islands just off Greece's western shore in the Ionian Sea had been settled by the Greeks at least as early as the 9th century BCE. The Republic of Venice gained control of the islands in the 13th century CE, followed by Venice in 1797, then France, and lastly, Britain. But Greek nationalist groups on the islands began pushing for *enosis* (incorporation into Greece). Finally, in 1864, the Great Powers transferred sovereignty of the islands to Greece, honoring King George I's request when he ascended Greece's throne.

The island of Crete was settled by the Minoans around 3500 BCE and was the earliest Bronze Age culture in the Greek world. Cretan revolutionaries could accurately say that Crete was and always had been an intrinsic part of the Greek world. The Cretans had opposed the Ottoman occupation, and now that King George I was titled "King of the Hellenes" (not just Greece), they declared Crete was part of the Kingdom of the Hellenes.

From 1866 to 1869, the Great Cretan Revolution raged against the Turks. The November 1866 Holocaust of Arkadi was an Ottoman attack on the Arkadi Monastery, the rebel headquarters. Hundreds of women and children had fled to the monastery for safety when the Ottomans began raiding their villages. But as the Greek rebels ran out of ammunition, the Turks' gigantic cannons blew down the monastery's gates on the second day of fighting.

The situation was hopeless. If the Cretans surrendered, the women would be raped, the children sold into slavery, and the men executed. The abbot called on the men to retreat to the monastery's vault where the gunpowder was stored and blow it up once the Turkish forces got inside. The explosion killed about 850 Greeks, including most of the women and children, and over 1,500 Turks.

The incident incited a passionate uproar throughout Europe and America, as the newspapers printed letters from French poet Victor Hugo describing the tragedy. People sent supplies to Crete and traveled there to help fight. Ottoman Grand Vizier Ali Pasha arrived in Crete in 1867 and reconquered Crete section by section but gave the Cretan Christians some local autonomy. By 1869, the rebels had either fled to Greece or submitted to Ottoman rule.

At the beginning of George I's reign, the new constitution instituted a single-chamber parliament and did away with the senate. King George could choose his prime minister, call for parliamentary sessions, and dissolve parliament if his cabinet endorsed his decree. For the first decade of George I's reign, his parliament was a disaster. George ignored public opinion when it came to his choices for prime minister and continually dissolved parliament.

Charilaos Trikoupis, a liberal leader of parliament, published an anonymous manifesto in the Athens newspaper in 1874 titled "Who's to Blame?" He criticized King George for frequently dissolving parliament and allowing multiple minority parties. He recommended the *dedilomeni* principle of parliamentary confidence: before a politician could be appointed prime minister, he must have majority support in parliament. He believed this system would force various factions to collaborate. Once Trikoupis admitted to authoring the article, King George invited him to form a government, declaring he would only appoint the leader of the parliament's majority party as prime minister.[45]

Greece continued to pursue annexing Thessaly and Epirus. When Russia and Turkey went to war in 1877, it provided a golden opportunity. George's sister Dagmar interceded with her father-in-law, Emperor Alexander II of Russia, asking him to ally with Greece in the war. But the other two Great Powers, Britain and France, would not permit Greece's involvement. Yet, when Russia won in 1878, and the Congress of Berlin met to hash out the new borders, Greece claimed Thessaly, Epirus, and Crete.[46] The British and French were favorable toward the idea, but the Ottoman Turks kept Crete and granted Thessaly and a section of Epirus to Greece in 1881.

The thirty-two-day Greco-Turkish War broke out in 1897 in Crete, which had always been a hotbed of dissent in the Ottoman Empire. As fighting erupted between the Ottoman Empire and

[45] Richard Clogg, *A Short History of Modern Greece* (Cambridge: Cambridge University Press, 1979), 86.

[46] Clogg, *Modern Greece*, 89.

Greece, the Great Powers surrounded the island with their ships, attempting to disrupt the conflict. Germany supported Turkey, which was awkward for King George since his son, Constantine, was married to Sophie, the German Kaiser's sister. Crown Prince Constantine was the general of the Greek forces when the fighting spread to Thessaly and Macedonia.

This was Greece's first war since its revolution. It was outmanned and outgunned and lost most of the battles. Nicholas II of Russia (Alexander III's son) mediated a peace treaty, which forced Greece to pay war reparations to Turkey. But the following year, the Great Powers removed the Ottomans and made Crete an autonomous state. King George's son, Prince George, served as high commissioner of the Cretan State for fifteen years until Crete formally became part of Greece in 1913.

In 1913, King George was looking forward to his Golden Jubilee in October, celebrating fifty years as king. He intended to abdicate after the ceremonies, with his son Constantine then taking the throne. But on March 18th, as he was enjoying an afternoon stroll in Athens, a mentally ill man shot him in the back at close range. The king died instantly. Constantine I succeeded him as the first Greek king born in Greece. He was also the first Greek king who was already a member of the Greek Orthodox Church.

Although King George I contended with multiple challenges, Greece became stabilized, gained territory, and improved its infrastructure during his long reign. In 1881, construction began on the Corinth Canal across the Isthmus of Corinth, linking the Saronic Gulf and the Gulf of Corinth: a shortcut between the Ionian and Aegean Seas. The ancient Greeks had dreamed of building the canal, and Roman Emperor Nero began construction in 67 CE, digging the first basketful of dirt. But he died several months later, and construction stopped. The Greeks finally completed the channel in 1893. It is still used by smaller vessels today, although it temporarily closed in October 2022 following catastrophic landslides.

King George also revived the Olympic Games, opening the first modern Olympics in 1896 in the Panathenaic Stadium of Athens. Crown Prince Constantine served as president of its organizing committee and raised the necessary funds to host the games. The

Panathenaic Stadium was built of marble in 144 CE, and businessman George Averoff paid 920,000 drachmas (about one million USD) for its restoration.[47] The stadium is still used today and served as an Olympic venue in 2004.

Greece had been isolated from the Renaissance during Ottoman rule, except for the Ionian islands and Crete, which had been under European control for part of the time. The Cretan School and Ionia's Heptanese School assimilated the European artistic revolution and combined Eastern and Western traditions. El Greco (Doménikos Theotokópoulos) trained at the Cretan School.

During the 19th-century reigns of Greece's first two monarchs, the country experienced a flourishing of the arts. Greek artists often studied in Munich and put their spin on Romanticism, incorporating Greece's landscapes, history, and revolutionary ideals. The works of this era display raw emotion and theatrics. Historical paintings feature the heroism and sacrifices of the Greek Revolution. In the latter half of the 19th century, historical themes gave way to depictions of everyday life and nature.

---

[47] David C. Young, *The Modern Olympics: A Struggle for Revival* (Baltimore: Johns Hopkins University Press, 1996), 128.

Chapter 12: Greece in the 20th Century

The Balkan Wars, which lit the fuse to World War I, erupted after years of simmering tensions among the Slavs and other ethnic groups within the Ottoman Empire. Worried about the Balkan powder keg and how a revolution might throw the rest of Europe out of balance, Europe's Great Powers used their diplomatic power to quell aspirations of a revolt.

But Greece had similarly suffered under the Ottoman Empire, and its people felt a sense of camaraderie with those still struggling for independence in the Balkans. In 1912, Greece and the Slavic states secretly formed the Balkan League, which consisted of Bulgaria, Serbia, Greece, and Montenegro. The alliance represented distinct ethnic groups that usually fought each other but joined forces against Turkey while it was distracted with Italy's invasion of Libya.

On October 5th, 1912, the first day of the war, Greek Lieutenant Dimitrios Kamberos flew a reconnaissance flight over Thessaly: history's first military aviation mission. Within one month, the Balkan alliance shocked the world by driving the Ottoman forces out of southeastern Europe. The Great Powers scrambled to regain control, calling everyone to London to sort out the Balkan's new boundaries. Finally, after sixty-three meetings, they hashed out a treaty ending the First Balkan War on May 30th, 1913.

The Bulgarians were displeased. Serbia and Greece had crushed Bulgaria's hopes of getting most of Macedonia by deciding to keep the territories their own forces had conquered. Exactly one month later, Bulgaria incited the Second Balkan War by launching a surprise attack on Greece and Serbia. Bulgaria ended up getting attacked on all sides when the Ottoman Empire jumped back into the fray, and Romania invaded Bulgaria's northern borders.

The war ended within six weeks, and this time, the players, rather than the Great Powers, negotiated the Treaty of Bucharest. Turkey regained Thrace in Bulgaria, and Serbia got northern Macedonia. Greece got southern Epirus and Macedonia, the Aegean Islands, and formal control of Crete, expanding to over twice its size. The Balkan Wars were notable for Greece's submarine *Delfin* launching the world's first torpedo attack (albeit unsuccessfully) against a warship: the Ottoman light cruiser *Mecidiye.*[48]

World War I detonated in 1914 after a Serbian nationalist, Gavrilo Princip, shot and killed Austria-Hungary's Crown Prince Franz Ferdinand and his wife, Sophie. Austria-Hungary declared war on Serbia, and multiple other nations jumped in. The war saw the Central Powers (Germany, Austria-Hungary, Bulgaria, and the Ottoman Empire) facing off against the Allied Powers (Great Britain, France, Russia, Italy, Romania, Canada, Japan, the United States, and eventually Greece).

Greece's treaty with Serbia at the end of the Balkan Wars promised mutual military assistance in the event of a third-party attack. But since the third party referred to Bulgaria, Prime Minister Eleftherios Venizelos advocated remaining neutral unless Bulgaria got involved. If that happened, which Venizelos thought likely, he promoted joining the Allied Powers.

But King Constantine I and his foreign ministers thought that Germany and the Central Powers would win the war and didn't want to be on the losing side. Moreover, the king had attended university in Germany, trained in the German Imperial Army, and

---

[48] E. R. Hooten, *Prelude to the First World War: The Balkan Wars 1912-1913* (Gloucestershire: Fonthill Media, 2014).

married Sophie, the German Kaiser's sister. Yet, his mother, Olga, was living in her native Russia, which was fighting against Germany. Constantine was in an awkward position and wanted to stay out of the war entirely.

Prime Minister Venizelos and King Constantine I.

In September 1915, Bulgaria invaded Serbia, so Prime Minister Venizelos mobilized the Greek troops to honor their treaty. Needing more men, Venizelos asked the French to send additional troops, which they did. But Venizelos failed to clear the matter with the king and parliament; consequently, King Constantine dismissed him. Alexandros Zaimis became the new prime minister, and he informed Serbia that Greece could not help.

King Constantine and the parliament desperately tried to remain neutral in the war but still suffered. The Allies blocked coal and wheat coming into Greece and seized the Greek islands of Lesbos and Corfu. The French took Greece's Fort Dova Tepe on the

Macedonian-Greek border. Two weeks later, the German-Bulgarian columns attacked and seized Greece's Rupel Fortress in central Macedonia. French General Maurice Sarrail imposed martial law in Thessaloniki, controlling all communications, railways, and the harbor. In June, the Allies commanded Greece to demobilize its military. Bulgaria invaded, occupying eastern Macedonia by late August 1916. In October, the Italians attacked and occupied Greek-held northern Epirus.

Enough was enough! Former Prime Minister Venizelos and many other exasperated Greeks formed a separate Greek government on October 9th: the Provisional Government of National Defense. They joined the Allies and declared war on Germany and Bulgaria. The Allied Powers insisted King Constantine abdicate, and when he left for Switzerland in June 1917, Greece's Provisional Government took control of the whole country. Greece routed Bulgaria from Macedonia and retook all of Serbia in tandem with the Allied Forces. World War I ended in November 1918, and Greece received Thrace through the ensuing treaties.

When the Allied Powers forced Constantine's abdication, they ruled out Crown Prince George as the next king, believing he shared his father's pro-German leanings. They permitted Constantine's second son, Alexander, to become Greece's king, though.[49] King Alexander ruled until his sudden death in October 1920 from a monkey bite. He was walking in the summer palace gardens when the gardener's Barbary macaque attacked the king's German shepherd. As the king tried to separate the animals, another monkey attacked him, leaving him with several bites that went septic. Three weeks later, the king died. At that point, Greece invited Constantine I to return, and he resumed his rule in December 1920.

By this time, Greece had already entered the Greco-Turkish War (1919–1922). After WWI ended, Greece staked its claim to Anatolia (Asia Minor or western Turkey), which had once been part

---

[49] "Downfall of King Constantine," *Current History* (1916-1940) 6, no. 1 (1917): 83-85. http://www.jstor.org/stable/45328408.

of the Byzantine Empire. The crumbling Ottoman Empire still had 2.5 million Greeks, even though the Muslims systematically killed hundreds of thousands of Greek Christians in Turkey during WWI.[50] Venizelos's goal of claiming Asia Minor was to expel the Ottoman rule "from those territories where the majority of the population consists of Greeks."[51]

Greece's military landed at Smyrna on Turkey's western coast in May 1919, which it had received in the 1918 Armistice of Mudros. The Greeks and Armenians in the region joined forces with the Greek military and quickly gained control of western Asia Minor. The Turks fought back with guerrilla warfare, and both sides committed ethnic atrocities against the local citizens caught in the warzone. The Greeks slaughtered Muslims, and the Muslims murdered Greek Orthodox citizens, forcing the survivors out of their villages and east to the Smyrna region.

In the two months between King Alexander's death and King Constantine's reinstatement, the Greeks voted out Venizelos, forcing him to leave the country. When they brought King Constantine back to the throne, the Allied Powers cut financial and military aid to Greece. Russia was in the midst of a civil war, but the Soviet faction provided munitions to the revolutionaries of the Turkish Nationalist Movement. In 1921, the Greeks suffered a bitter defeat at the Battle of the Sakarya, losing 80 percent of its officers. In August 1922, the Turkish Great Offensive pushed forward with more than 100,000 soldiers. The Greeks had twice as many men but were disorganized and demoralized. The Turks crushed the Greek army, capturing fifteen thousand soldiers and forcing a retreat to the Aegean Sea.

The Turks burned down the Greek and Armenian sections of Smyrna. Trapped between the Turkish forces, the fire, and the sea, the frantic citizens had nowhere to flee. Nearly 100,000 people died as the city burned for nine days. The Allies decided a population exchange was the only way to end further atrocities. The 1923

---

[50] Adam Jones, *Genocide: A Comprehensive Introduction* (London: Routledge, 2006), 154-55.

[51] "Not War Against Islam – Statement by Greek Prime Minister," *The Scotsman.* June 29, 1920, 5, 29.

Treaty of Lausanne forced 1.2 million Orthodox Christians to leave Turkey for Greece and moved 400,000 Greek Muslims from Greece to Turkey.

The September 1922 burning of Smyrna.

Following the catastrophe at Smyrna, Venizelos's supporters compelled King Constantine I to abdicate again in September 1922, installing his oldest son, George II, as monarch. But when the Liberal Party came into power two years later, they exiled George, declaring Greece to be a republic. The new government threatened a minimum six-month jail sentence for anyone advocating a return to a monarchy or questioning the election results. The fragile new government limped along, interrupted by a one-year dictatorship when General Theodoros Pangalos staged a coup in 1925. He was ejected the following year, and the republic was restored. Venizelos regained control in 1928, bringing a measure of stability. Yet, the Great Depression (1929–1939) crushed Greece economically, and political chaos resumed.

The Greeks voted Venizelos out in 1932, and three military coups rocked the country between 1933 and 1935. Finally, in October 1935, General Georgios Kondylis forced himself into the position of prime minister, dissolved the republic, and staged a rigged election that restored the monarchy with 98 percent of the vote. George II, who had been living in two rooms at Brown's Hotel of London, returned to Greece in November 1935. Refusing to be a puppet king, he immediately butted heads with Kondylis, dismissed him, and appointed Konstantinos Demertzis as prime minister.

Demertzis dropped dead of a heart attack four months later, so George appointed Minister of Defense Ioannis Metaxas as the new prime minister. This appointment was highly unpopular among the rising Communist Party, and workers went on strike throughout Greece. Metaxas declared a state of emergency in August 1936, citing industrial unrest and the "communist danger." He disbanded parliament and formed the totalitarian August Regime, imitating Benito Mussolini's fascist Italy. He banned political parties and strikes and censored the media. His dictatorship remained in power for five years until his death in 1941.

As World War II loomed, Metaxas strengthened fortifications at the Bulgaria-Greece border with tunnels, machine-gun nests, and "dragon's teeth" structures to impede tanks. Mussolini's Italian forces invaded northwest Greece in October 1940, officially bringing Greece into World War II. The Greeks resisted with fierce tenacity and chased the Italians out of the country. In April 1941, three months after Metaxas died, Adolf Hitler invaded Greece. The king and parliament fled to Crete as Germans, Bulgarians, and Italians swamped Greece.

The occupying forces plundered the farms and requisitioned food to feed their troops. Greece had always required grain shipments from outside the country for its population; the Allies' blockade now cut that off. As the Great Famine set in, dead bodies littered the streets of Athens, with as many as one thousand dying of starvation each day. The situation in other towns and cities was just as bleak, with an estimated 5 percent of Greece's population starving to death.

But Greece had relied on resistance forces in its rugged mountains during the Greek War of Independence, and similar mountain guerilla troops launched a successful defense against the invaders. Italy surrendered to the Allies in 1943, the Germans and Bulgarians withdrew from Greece in 1944, and the Greek king and government returned to Greece. World War II ended in September 1945.

A cavalry brigade of the Greek People's Liberation Army.
https://commons.wikimedia.org/wiki/File:IPPIKO-ELAS-1.jpg

Greece's two largest resistance movements—the National Liberation Front and the Greek People's Liberation Army—were communist and backed by the Soviet Union and Yugoslavia. Their clash with Greece's government exploded into the Greek Civil War, which lasted from 1944 to 1949 and wreaked even more devastation on the war-torn country. The civil war killed 100,000 people and mangled the economy, which was already on the brink of ruin. Finally, Soviet Union's Joseph Stalin told the Greek communists to fold up their operations; it would be too hard to fight Britain and the United States. One positive aspect of the liberal influence in Greece was women finally getting the right to vote on May 28th, 1952.

After World War II, the Dodecanese Islands in the Aegean and Mediterranean Seas went to Greece with the stipulation that they remain demilitarized. The Minoans and Myceneans had settled the islands beginning in the 2nd millennium BCE, and they had always had close ties to Greece. During the 20th century, the islands passed through the hands of Italy, Germany, and Britain before uniting with Greece on March 7th, 1948.

In the 2nd millennium BCE, the Myceneans also settled the island of Cyprus in the eastern Mediterranean Sea, south of Turkey and west of Syria. In the 20th century, about 80 percent of the population was Cypriot-Greek-speaking people of Greek lineage who belonged to the Greek Orthodox Church. The Ottoman Empire occupied Cyprus until the Russo-Turkish War (1877–1878), when Britain took over its administration.

In the 20th century, the Greek population of Cyprus pressed for a union with Greece, which the ethnic Turks resisted. When Cyprus gained independence in 1960, the Cypriot Turks, who consisted of 20 percent of the population, got 30 percent representation in parliament. Many Greeks considered this overrepresentation. In 1963, violence broke out, with 174 Greeks and 364 Turks dying. The Greeks destroyed 109 Turkish villages, displacing 30,000 ethnic Turks. In 1974, the Cypriot Greeks staged a coup, still desiring to unite with Greece, which triggered a Turkish invasion. The end result was a line dividing the island into a northern section under Turkish rule and a southern section under Cypriot-Greek control.

In mainland Greece, the struggle between the communist-leaning liberals and right-wing conservatives reached the boiling point in 1967. The United States had inserted itself in 1947 with the Truman Doctrine, which supported an authoritarian government in Greece to guard against Soviet influence. In the 1964 election, the more progressive Centre Union Party won a landslide victory, with its founder, Georgios Papandreou, becoming Greece's new prime minister.

Papandreou wanted to weed out military officers involved in the CIA-funded, anti-communist IDEA society (*Ieros Desmos Ellinon Axiomatikon* or Holy Bond of Greek Officers), which advocated a dictatorship. When twenty-four-year-old Constantine II ascended the throne in 1964, he clashed with Papandreou, forcing his resignation in 1965. The king replaced Papandreou with a series of prime ministers from the Centre Union Party, which still held the majority, but none served more than a few weeks. Papandreou's supporters considered these men to be defectors or "apostates" from the party, labeling Constantine's actions the *Apostasia* or Royal Coup.

Greece stumbled through this political crisis. On April 21st, 1967, the people of Athens awakened to the sound of gunfire and tanks rolling into the city. Military songs blared on the radio, followed by the announcement, "The Hellenic Armed Forces have taken the country's governance." Right-wing military officers had staged a coup called the Greek Junta, which established a seven-year dictatorship. They censored the media and arrested left-wing politicians and ten thousand blacklisted citizens, sending them to prison or a concentration camp on Yaros Island. Thousands endured torture by the Security Police and Greek Military Police.

King Constantine attempted a counter-coup in December 1967 with the navy and air force members that were still loyal to him. When the coup failed, he fled Greece with his family, and the junta appointed Major Georgios Zoitakis as regent in the king's absence. Zoitakis appointed Colonel George Papadopoulos, one of the coup's three ringleaders, as prime minister. In 1972, Papadopoulos became the joint regent and prime minister and abolished the monarchy in June 1973.

In November 1973, several hundred students launched a protest at Athens's National Technical University, demanding the military junta abandon power. The next day, thousands of citizens poured onto the campus to support the student protestors. The students constructed a radio system that broadcasted throughout Athens. Three days later, a tank crashed through the university's gates, and the military brutally cleared out the protestors.

The following week, Dimitrios Ioannidis, Papadopoulos's protégé, initiated a counter-coup that ejected Papadopoulos, accusing him of straying from the 1967 revolutionary ideals. But the Greek military pulled support from Ioannidis when he sponsored the disastrous 1974 coup in Cyprus, which resulted in Turkey invading the island. The second-generation junta leadership decided to put Greece back on track for elections. They invited Konstantinos Karamanlis, who had served as prime minister in the early 1960s, to return from exile and serve as Greece's interim leader until elections resumed.

With elections restored and a new administration in place, Constantine II confidently expected to return as Greece's monarch. However, the electorate voted against restoring the monarchy. Constantine remained in London, as he was a close friend of his cousin Prince Charles (now King Charles III) and godfather of William, Prince of Wales. In 2013, Greece finally permitted Constantine to return to live in Greece as a private citizen.

On January 1st, 1981, Greece joined the European Economic Community (EEC), to which it had first applied in 1959. In 1961, Greece and the EEC signed an Association Agreement, but the ensuing political chaos froze the process. With democracy restored in 1974, Prime Minister Karamanlis reactivated the procedures to integrate Greece as a full member of the European Union. His goal was to restore economic and political stability and modernize Greek society. Greece adopted the single currency euro in 2002.

In August 2004, Athens again hosted the Olympic Games in its twenty-fifth competition since King George I revived the modern games in 1896. Athens built a new airport, ring road, and subway system to welcome over eleven thousand competitors and an estimated one million visitors. Despite the media's dire predictions, all the venues were completed on schedule, and the transportation systems and venues awed everyone. "Unforgettable dream games!" exclaimed President Jacques Rogge of the International Olympic Committee.

Conclusion

Greece immensely impacted our world as the cradle of Western civilization. The Minoans were the first advanced European culture, a people who built breathtaking palaces, created dazzling art, and devised Europe's first two written languages. The Myceneans followed soon after, elevating Greece and its surrounding islands to new levels of urban organization, engineering, architecture, and warfare proficiency. Their ships sailed around the Mediterranean and Black Seas, exchanging goods, establishing colonies, and spreading an advanced culture.

After Greece's Dark Ages, the archaic era emerged to introduce Europe to written literature, such as Homer's *Iliad* and *Odyssey*. We are indebted to the ancient Greeks' stunning breakthroughs in mathematics, science, and medicine. Greek philosophers developed a logical observation of the physical world, and early Greek physicians devised the systematic diagnosis of common diseases. Greece left an indelible stamp on Roman culture, the Christian Church, the Byzantine Empire, the Renaissance, and modern-day politics. Greece's experimentation and development of political systems contributed enormously to democratic republics worldwide.

Cretan hieroglyphs and Linear A used in Crete and southern Greece were the first European writing systems. Tablets with Linear B dating to at least 1350 BCE document an ancient form of the Greek language still spoken today. Spoken and written Koine Greek dates to the 4th century BCE and became the lingua franca of the vast territories covering three continents conquered by Alexander the Great. Scholars translated the Hebrew Tanakh (Old Testament) into Koine Greek (the Septuagint version) in Hellenistic Egypt, and the apostles wrote the New Testament in Koine Greek.

The Byzantine Empire left an enduring legacy, especially its contribution to developing the Eastern Orthodox Church. Byzantine architecture spread to Russia and south to Egypt. Byzantine monks, philosophers, and artists cultivated a unique cultural blend of Christianity with Greek philosophy, science, art, and literature. They preserved Greek and Roman art, literature, philosophy, science, technology, and law through the centuries until the Renaissance.

Modern Greece has trailblazed through multiple challenges, employing innovations and silencing doubters. After freeing itself from Ottoman rule, Greece established the oldest parliamentary democracy in the eastern Mediterranean and southeast Europe. It has endured since 1864, with three brief non-democratic regimes lasting a combined total of twenty-three years. With a few bumps along the way, Greece has emerged from abject poverty to economic prosperity in the past seven decades. While its ancient classical past is an intrinsic element of Greece's national identity, the nation is a world player today, developing an impressive geopolitical identity in the eastern Mediterranean.

Here's another book by Enthralling History that you might like

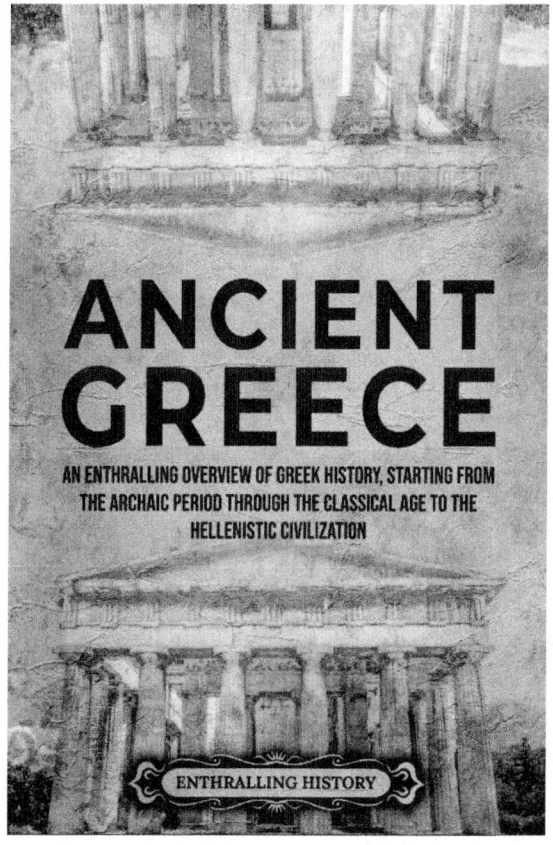

Free limited time bonus

Stop for a moment. We have a free bonus set up for you. The problem is this: we forget 90% of everything that we read after 7 days. Crazy fact, right? Here's the solution: we've created a printable, 1-page pdf summary for this book that you're reading now. All you have to do to get your free pdf summary is to go to the following website: **https://livetolearn.lpages.co/enthrallinghistory/**

Once you do, it will be intuitive. Enjoy, and thank you!

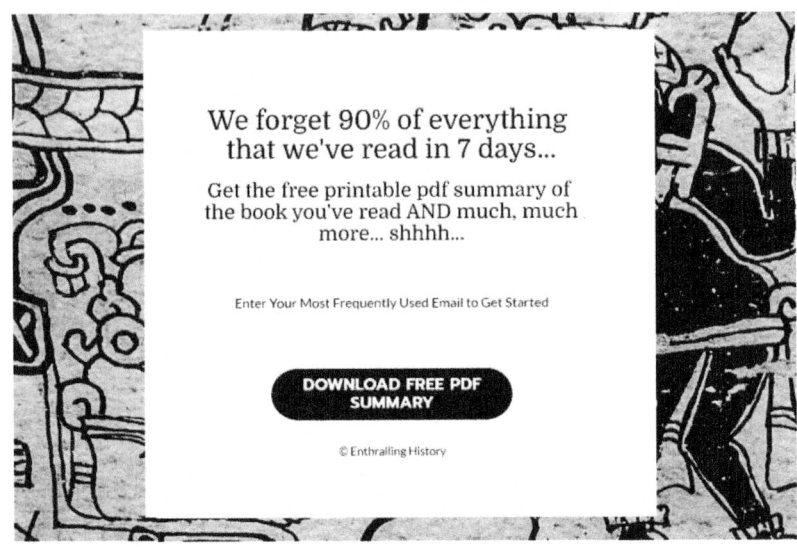

Bibliography

Arrian. *Alexander the Great: The Anabasis and the Indica.* Translated by Martin Hammond. Oxford: Oxford University Press, 2013.

Austin, M. M. "Greek Tyrants and the Persians, 546-479 B. C." *The Classical Quarterly* 40, no. 2 (1990): 289-306. http://www.jstor.org/stable/639090

Barron, John P. "The Sixth-Century Tyranny at Samos." *The Classical Quarterly* 14, no. 2 (1964): 210-29. http://www.jstor.org/stable/637725.

Beck, Julien, Despina Koutsoumbab, Dimitris Sakellariouc, Morgane Surdez, Flavio Anselmettie, Nikos Papadopoulos, Ionnis Morfis, et al. "Searching for Neolithic Sites in the Bay of Kiladha, Greece." *Quaternary International* 584 (May 20, 2021):129-40. https://www.sciencedirect.com/science/article/pii/S1040618220308466#

Bennett, Bob, and Mike Roberts. *The Wars of Alexander's Successors, 323-281 BC. Volume I: Commanders and Campaigns.* South Yorkshire: Pen & Sword Military, 2019.

Bennett, Bob, and Mike Roberts. *The Wars of Alexander's Successors 323 - 281 BC. Volume 2: Battles and Tactics.* South Yorkshire: Pen & Sword Military, 2019.

Bicknell, P.J. "Anaximenes' Astronomy." *Acta Classica* 12 (1969): 53–85. http://www.jstor.org/stable/24591168.

Cartledge, Paul. *The Spartans: The World of the Warrior-Heroes of Ancient Greece.* New York: The Overlook Press, 2003.

Castleden, Rodney. *The Knossos Labyrinth: A New View of the 'Palace of Minos' at Knossos.* London: Routledge, 2012.

Chioti, Lamprini. "The Herulian Invasion in Athens (267 CE). The Archaeological Evidence." *Destructions, Survival, and Recovery in Ancient Greece*. American School of Classical Studies at Athens: May 16, 2019.
https://www.academia.edu/39196609/The_Herulian_invasion_in_Athens_267_CE_The_Archaeological_Evidence

Clogg, Richard. *A Concise History of Greece*. Cambridge: Cambridge University Press, 2021.

Clogg, Richard. *A Short History of Modern Greece*. Cambridge: Cambridge University Press, 1979.

Coleman, John E. "The Chronology and Interconnections of the Cycladic Islands in the Neolithic Period and the Early Bronze Age." *American Journal of Archaeology* 78, no. 4 (1974): 333–44.
https://doi.org/10.2307/502747.

Daskalov, Roumen, and Tchavdar Marinov. *Entangled Histories of the Balkans - Volume One: National Ideologies and Language Policies*. Leiden: Brill, 2013.

Davies, Siriol, and Jack L. Davis. "Greeks, Venice, and the Ottoman Empire." *Hesperia Supplements* 40 (2007): 25–31.
http://www.jstor.org/stable/20066763.

Dillon, John and Lloyd P. Gerson. *Neoplatonic Philosophy: Introductory Readings*. Cambridge, MA: Hackett Publishing Company, 2004.

"Downfall of King Constantine." *Current History* (1916-1940) 6, no. 1 (1917): 83–85. http://www.jstor.org/stable/45328408.

Figueira, Thomas J. "Population Patterns in Late Archaic and Classical Sparta." *Transactions of the American Philological Association* 116 (1986): 165–213. https://doi.org/10.2307/283916.

Gellius, A. Cornelius. *Noctes Atticae (Attic Nights)*. Volume I, Book III. Loeb Classical Library.
http://penelope.uchicago.edu/Thayer/E/Roman/Texts/Gellius/3*.html#8

Guthrie, W. K. C. *A History of Greek Philosophy*. Cambridge: Cambridge University Press, 1979.

Guthrie, W. K. C. *The Sophists*. Cambridge: Cambridge University Press, 1977.

Hack, Harold M. "Thebes and the Spartan Hegemony, 386-382 B.C." *The American Journal of Philology* 99, no. 2 (1978): 210–27.
https://doi.org/10.2307/293647.

Heidel, William Arthur. "Anaximander's Book, the Earliest Known Geographical Treatise." *Proceedings of the American Academy of Arts and Sciences* 56, no. 7 (1921): 239-88. doi:10.2307/20025852.

Henderson, W.J. "The Nature and Function of Solon's Poetry: Fr. Diehl, 4 West." *Acta Classica* 25 (1982): 21-33. http://www.jstor.org/stable/24591787.

Herodotus, *The Histories.* Translated by George Rawlinson. New York: Dutton & Co, 1862. http://classics.mit.edu/Herodotus/history.html

Hofmanová, Zuzana, Susanne Kreutzer, Garrett Hellenthal, Christian Sell, Yoan Diekmann, David Díez-del-Molino, Lucy van Dorp, et al. "Early Farmers from across Europe Directly Descended from Neolithic Aegeans." *PNAS.* 113 (25) (June 6, 2016): 6886–6891. doi:10.1073/pnas.1523951113. ISSN 0027-8424. PMC 4922144. PMID 27274049.

Homer. *The Iliad.* Translated by Samuel Butler. Internet Classics Archive. http://classics.mit.edu/Homer/iliad.html

Homer. *The Odyssey.* Translated by Samuel Butler. Internet Classics Archive. http://classics.mit.edu/Homer/odyssey.html

Hooten, E.R. *Prelude to the First World War: The Balkan Wars 1912-1913.* Gloucestershire: Fonthill Media, 2014.

Isocrates. *Letters.* Perseus Digital Library. Tufts University. http://www.perseus.tufts.edu/hopper/text?doc=Perseus:text:1999.01.0246:letter=3.

Jenkins, Romilly J. H. "The Hellenistic Origins of Byzantine Literature." Dumbarton Oaks Papers 17 (1963): 37–52. https://doi.org/10.2307/1291189.

Jones, Adam. *Genocide: A Comprehensive Introduction.* London: Routledge, 2006.

Jones, A. H. M. "The Greeks under the Roman Empire." *Dumbarton Oaks Papers* 17 (1963): 1–19. https://doi.org/10.2307/1291187.

Josephus, Flavius. *Antiquities of the Jews.* Translated by William Whiston. Project Gutenberg. https://www.gutenberg.org/files/2848/2848-h/2848-h.htm

Kaldellis, Anthony. *Hellenism in Byzantium: The Transformations of Greek Identity and the Reception of the Classical Tradition.* Cambridge: Cambridge University Press, 2007.

Kelder, Jorrit M. (2010). *The Kingdom of Mycenae: A Great Kingdom in the Late Bronze Age Aegean.* Bethesda: CDL Press, 2010

King, RJ, S. S. Ozcan, T. Carter, E. Kalfoğlu, S. Atasoy, C. Triantaphyllidis, A. Couva's, et al. "Differential Y-chromosome Anatolian Influences on the Greek and Cretan Neolithic." *Annals of Human Genetics.* 72 (March 2008): 205-14. do: 10.1111/j.1469-1809.2007.00414.x. PMID: 18269686.

Krausmüller, Dirk. "Emperors, Patriarchs, Metropolitans, Deacons and Monks: Individuals and Groups in the Byzantine Church (6th–11th Centuries)." *Scrinium* 17, 1 (2021): 199-238, doi: https://doi.org/10.1163/18177565-bja10048

Lazaridis, I, A. Mittnik, N. Patterson, S. Mallick, N. Rohland, S. Pfrengle, A. Furtwängler, et al. "Genetic Origins of the Minoans and Mycenaeans." *Nature* 548 (August 10, 2017): 214-18. doi: 10.1038/nature23310. Epub 2017 Aug 2. PMID: 28783727; PMCID: PMC5565772.

Lupack, Susan. "Mycenaean Religion." In *The Oxford Handbook of the Bronze Age Aegean,* edited by Eric H. Cline, 2012. 10.1093/oxfordhb/9780199873609.013.0020.

Mansfield, D. F. "Plimpton 322: A Study of Rectangles." *Foundations of Science* 26 (2021): 977–1005. https://doi.org/10.1007/s10699-021-09806-0

Martin, Thomas R. *Ancient Greece: From Prehistoric to Hellenistic Times.* New Haven: Yale University Press, 1996.

Matyszak, Philip. *Greece Against Rome: The Fall of the Hellenistic Kingdoms 250–31 BC.* South Yorkshire: Pen & Sword Military, 2020.

Matyszak, Philip. *The Rise of the Hellenistic Kingdoms, 336–250 BC.* South Yorkshire: Pen & Sword Military, 2019.

Mazower, Mark. *The Greek Revolution: 1821 and the Making of Modern Europe.* New York: Penguin Press, 2021.

Mittal, Rakesh. *Hellenism and the Shaping of the Byzantine Empire.* Marquette University, 2010. https://epublications.marquette.edu/cgi/viewcontent.cgi?article=1001&context=jablonowski_award

"Not War Against Islam – Statement by Greek Prime Minister." *The Scotsman.* June 29, 1920.

Ostrogorsky, George. "Byzantine Cities in the Early Middle Ages." *Dumbarton Oaks Papers* 13 (1959): 45–66. https://doi.org/10.2307/1291128.

Oost, Stewart Irvin. "Cypselus the Bacchiad." *Classical Philology* 67, no. 1 (1972): 10-30. http://www.jstor.org/stable/269012.

Peoples, R. Scott. *Crusade of Kings.* Rockville, MD: Wildside Press LLC, 2013, 13. ISBN 978-0-8095-7221-2

Plato. *The Republic.* Translated by Benjamin Jowett. Internet Classics Archive. http://classics.mit.edu/Plato/republic.9.viii.html

Plutarch. *Cimon.* Translated by John Dryden. Internet Classics Archive. http://classics.mit.edu/Plutarch/cimon.html

Polybius. *Histories.* Book 16. http://www.perseus.tufts.edu/hopper/text?doc=Perseus%3Atext%3A1999.01.0234%3Abook%3D16%3Achapter%3D34

Pomeroy, Sarah B., Stanley M. Burstein, Walter Donlan, Jennifer Tolbert Roberts, David W. Tandy, and Georgia Tsouvala. *Ancient Greece: Politics, Society, and Culture.* New York: Oxford University Press, 2020.

Rhodes, P. J. *Athenian Democracy* (Edinburgh Readings on the Ancient World). Oxford: Oxford University Press, 2004.

Runciman, Steven. *The Byzantine Theocracy: The Weil Lectures, Cincinnati* (Cambridge: Cambridge University Press, 2004), ISBN 978-0-521-54591-4.

Runnels, Curtis. "Review of Aegean Prehistory IV: The Stone Age of Greece from the Paleolithic to the Advent of the Neolithic." *American Journal of Archaeology* 99, no. 4 (1995): 699–728. https://doi.org/10.2307/506190.

Svolopoulos, Constantinos. "The Ecumenical Patriarchate in the Ottoman Empire (1453-1923): Adaptation and Change." *Journal of Modern Hellenism.* 17-18 (2000-2001); 107-123.

Syme, Ronald. "The Greeks under Roman Rule." *Proceedings of the Massachusetts Historical Society* 72 (1957): 3–20. http://www.jstor.org/stable/25080512.

Theophrastus. *Characters.* Translated by R.C. Jebb. https://www.eudaemonist.com/biblion/characters/

The William Davidson Talmud (Koren - Steinsaltz). https://www.sefaria.org/Yoma.69a.14?lang=bi&with=all&lang2=en

Thucydides. *History of the Peloponnesian War.* Translated by Rex Warner. New York: Penguin Classics, 1972.

Treadgold, Warren. "The Persistence of Byzantium." *The Wilson Quarterly* (1976-) 22, no. 4 (1998): 66–91. http://www.jstor.org/stable/40260386.

Warren, Peter. "Knossos: New Excavations and Discoveries," *Archaeology* 37, no. 4 (1984): 48–55. http://www.jstor.org/stable/41731580.

Worthington, Ian. *By the Spear: Philip II, Alexander the Great, and the Rise and Fall of the Macedonian Empire* (Ancient Warfare and Civilization). Oxford: Oxford University Press, 2016.

Xenophon. *The Landmark Xenophon's Hellenika*. Translated by John Marincola. New York: Anchor, 2010.

Young, David C. *The Modern Olympics: A Struggle for Revival*. Baltimore: Johns Hopkins University Press, 1996.

Printed in Great Britain
by Amazon

44902603R00089